TEACHER'S PET PUBLICATIONS

LITPLAN TEACHER PACK
for
Things Fall Apart
based on the book by
Chinua Achebe

Written by
Barbara M. Linde, MA Ed.

© 1995 Teacher's Pet Publications
All Rights Reserved

This **LitPlan** for Chinua Achebe's
Things Fall Apart
has been brought to you by Teacher's Pet Publications, Inc.

Copyright Teacher's Pet Publications 1995
11504 Hammock Point
Berlin MD 21811

Only the student materials in this unit plan (such as worksheets, study questions, and tests) may be reproduced multiple times for use in the purchaser's classroom. No other portion of this unit plan may be reproduced in any way without written consent of Teacher's Pet Publications.

For any additional copyright questions,
contact Teacher's Pet Publications.

www.tpet.com

TABLE OF CONTENTS - *Things Fall Apart*

Introduction	5
Unit Objectives	7
Unit Outline	8
Reading Assignment Sheet	9
Study Questions	13
Quiz/Study Questions (Multiple Choice)	24
Pre-Reading Vocabulary Worksheets	41
Lesson One (Introductory Lesson)	57
Nonfiction Assignment Sheet	60
Oral Reading Evaluation Form	62
Writing Assignment 1	64
Writing Evaluation Form	65
Writing Assignment 2	67
Extra Writing Assignments/Discussion ?s	69
Writing Assignment 3	75
Vocabulary Review Activities	76
Unit Review Activities	77
Unit Tests	83
Vocabulary Resource Materials	117
Unit Resource Materials	131

A FEW NOTES ABOUT THE AUTHOR
CHINUA ACHEBE

ACHEBE, Chinua 1930

Chinua Achebe was born on November 16, 1930, in Ogidi, Nigeria. He was raised in this traditional village, although his parents were Christians. Achebe considers himself part of a generation that is in transition between the old village ways and the modern world.

Mr. Achebe began his career with the Nigerian Broadcasting Corporation, where he worked from 1954-1966. After that he became a senior research fellow at the University of Nigeria, Nsukka, and then a professor of English. From 1972-75 he was a visiting professor of English at the University of Massachusetts, and was a visiting professor of English at the University of Connecticut in 1975-76.

Things Fall Apart was his first novel, published in 1958. This novel established him as a major contemporary novelist. Many adult and children's books followed his first success: *No Longer at Ease* (1960), *The Sacrificial Egg and Other Stories* (1962), *Arrow of God* (1964), *A Man of People* (1966), *Chike and the River* (1966), *Beware Soul-Brother and Other Poems* (1971), *The Insider: Stories of War and Peace from Nigeria* (1971), *How the Leopard Got His Claws* (1972), *Girls at War and Other Stories* (1973), *Morning Yet on Creation Day* (1975), *The Flute* (1977), and *The Drum* (1977). Achebe is also the founding editor of the African Writers series published by Heinemann Books.

Chike and the River, published in 1966, was his first children's novel. It is about the adventures of a young boy. *The Flute* is a retelling of a traditional African folktale with some added details. *How the Leopard Got His Claws* is an animal fable which he wrote during the Biafran War.

Chinua Achebe has received many awards, including The Nigerian National Merit Award for intellectual achievement (1970), the Commonwealth Poetry Prize (1974), and the Lotus Award for Afro-Asian Writers (1975). He has honorary degrees from universities in the United States, Scotland, England, Canada, and Nigeria.

Mr. Achebe now lives in New York with his wife and four children. He and his wife both teach at Bard College.

INTRODUCTION-*Things Fall Apart*

This unit has been designed to develop students' reading, writing, thinking, listening and speaking skills through exercises and activities related to *Things Fall Apart* by Chinua Achebe. It includes seventeen lessons, supported by extra resource materials.

The **introductory lesson** introduces students to the novel through the use of a KWL worksheet. Students are also given the materials they will use during this unit and are shown how to use these materials.

The **reading assignments** are approximately thirty pages each; some are a little shorter while others are a little longer. Students have approximately 15 minutes of pre-reading work to do prior to each reading assignment. This pre-reading work involves reviewing the study questions for the assignment and doing some vocabulary work for 8 to 10 vocabulary words they will encounter in their reading.

The **study guide questions** are fact-based questions; students can find the answers to these questions right in the text. These questions come in two formats: short answer or multiple choice. The best use of these materials is probably to use the short answer version of the questions as study guides for students (since answers will be more complete), and to use the multiple choice version for occasional quizzes. It might be a good idea to make transparencies of your answer keys for the overhead projector.

The **vocabulary work** is intended to enrich students' vocabularies as well as to aid in the students' understanding of the book. Prior to each reading assignment, students will complete a two-part worksheet for approximately 8 to 10 vocabulary words in the upcoming reading assignment. Part I focuses on students' use of general knowledge and contextual clues by giving the sentence in which the word appears in the text. Students are then to write down what they think the words mean based on the words' usage. Part II gives students dictionary definitions of the words and has them match the words to the correct definitions based on the words' contextual usage. Students should then have an understanding of the words when they meet them in the text.

After each reading assignment, students will go back and formulate answers for the study guide questions. Discussion of these questions serves as a **review** of the most important events and ideas presented in the reading assignments.

After students complete extra discussion questions, there is a **vocabulary review** lesson which pulls together all of the separate vocabulary lists for the reading assignments and gives students a review of all of the words they have studied.

Following the reading of the book, two lessons are devoted to the **extra discussion questions/writing assignments.** These questions focus on interpretation, critical analysis and personal response, employing a variety of thinking skills and adding to the students' understanding of the novel. These questions are done as a **group activity.** Using the information they have acquired so far through individual work and class discussions, students get together to further examine the text and to brainstorm ideas relating to the themes of the novel.

The group activity is followed by a **reports and discussion** session in which the groups share their ideas about the book with the entire class; thus, the entire class gets exposed to many different ideas regarding the themes and events of the book.

There are three **writing assignments** in this unit, each with the purpose of informing, persuading, or having students express personal opinions. The first assignment is to **persuade**: students will take the role of a young clan member who wants to make a change in the way something is done. The second assignment is to **inform**: students will write a report from the point of view of the missionary. The third assignment is to express a personal **opinion**: students will write about a change in their own lives and how it affected them.

In addition, there is a **nonfiction reading assignment**. Students are required to read a piece of nonfiction related in some way to *Things Fall Apart*. After reading their nonfiction pieces, students will fill out a worksheet on which they answer questions regarding facts, interpretation, criticism, and personal opinions. During one class period, students make **oral presentations** about the nonfiction pieces they have read. This not only exposes all students to a wealth of information, it also gives students the opportunity to practice **public speaking.**

The **review lesson** pulls together all of the aspects of the unit. The teacher is given four or five choices of activities or games to use which all serve the same basic function of reviewing all of the information presented in the unit.

The **unit test** comes in two formats: all multiple choice-matching-true/false or a mixture of matching, short answer, and composition. As a convenience, two different tests for each format have been included.

There are additional **support materials** included with this unit. The **unit resource section** includes suggestions for an in-class library, crossword and word search puzzles related to the novel, and extra vocabulary worksheets. There is a list of **bulletin board ideas** which gives the teacher suggestions for bulletin boards to go along with this unit. In addition, there is a list of **extra class activities** the teacher could choose from to enhance the unit or as a substitution for an exercise the teacher might feel is inappropriate for his/her class. **Answer keys** are located directly after the **reproducible student materials** throughout the unit. The student materials may be reproduced for use in the teacher's classroom without infringement of copyrights. No other portion of this unit may be reproduced without the written consent of Teacher's Pet Publications, Inc.

UNIT OBJECTIVES-*Things Fall Apart*

1. Through reading *Things Fall Apart*, students will analyze characters and their situations to better understand the themes of the novel.

2. Students will demonstrate their understanding of the text on four levels: actual, interpretive, critical, and personal.

3. Students will practice reading aloud and silently to improve their skills in each area.

4. Students will enrich their vocabularies and improve their understanding of the autobiography through the vocabulary lessons prepared for use in conjunction with it.

5. Students will answer questions to demonstrate their knowledge and understanding of the main events and characters in *Things Fall Apart*.

6. Students will practice writing through a variety of writing assignments.

7. The writing assignments in this are geared to several purposes:
    a. To check the students' reading comprehension
    b. To make students think about the ideas presented by the novel
    c. To make students put those ideas into perspective
    d. To encourage critical and logical thinking
    e. To provide the opportunity to practice good grammar and improve students' use of the English language.

8. Students will read aloud, report, and participate in large and small group discussions to improve their public speaking and personal interaction skills.

UNIT OUTLINE - *Things Fall Apart*

1 Introduction PV 1-4	2 Read 1-4 Study ?s 1-4	3 PVR 5-7 Oral Reading Evaluation	4 Quiz 1-7 PVR 8-10	5 Writing Assignment 1
6 Study ?s 8-10 PVR 11-13	7 Study ?s 11-13 PVR 14-19	8 Study ?s 14-19 Writing Assignment 2	9 Writing Conferences	10 PVR 20-25 Study ?s 20-25
11 Extra Discussion Questions	12 Writing Assignment 3	13 Library Work	14 Nonfiction Assignment	15 Vocabulary Review
16 Unit Review	17 Test			

P= Preview Study Questions   V=Do Vocabulary Worksheet   R=Read

READING ASSIGNMENT SHEET-*Things Fall Apart*

Date Assigned	Assignment	Completion Date
	Part One, Chapters 1-4	
	Part One, Chapters 5-7	
	Part One, Chapters 8-10	
	Part One, Chapters 11-13	
	Part Two, Chapters 14-19	
	Part Two, Chapters 20-25	

STUDY GUIDE QUESTIONS

SHORT ANSWER STUDY QUESTIONS-*Things Fall Apart*

Chapters 1-4
1. Why was Okonkwo famous?
2. Describe Unoka.
3. Why had the men of Umuofia called a meeting?
4. Where does the story take place?
5. What influence did the oracle have on decisions made in Umuofia?
6. What were Okonkwo's greatest fear and greatest passion?
7. What upset Okonkwo most about his son, Nwoye?
8. What did Okonkwo bring home from his trip to Mbaino?
9. How did Okonkwo begin his prosperous career?
10. How did Ikemefuna react to living with Okonkwo's family?
11. What unheard of thing did Okonkwo do during the Week of Peace?
12. How did the people view yams?

Chapters 5-7
1. Describe the Feast of the New Yam.
2. Who was Okonkwo's favorite child, and what did he often say about the child?
3. What unacceptable thing did Okonkso do just before the Feast of the New Yam?
4. Who was Chielo, and why was she important?
5. What sport did the villagers enjoy watching during their feasting?
6. What influence did Ikemefuna have on Nwoye?
7. How did Okonkwo feel about Ikemefuna's influence on Nwoye?
8. How did the villagers feel about the coming of the locusts, and what did they do about it?
9. What did the village decide to do with Ikemefuna?
10. Who struck the last blow to Ikemefuna, and why?

Chapters 8-10
1. What did Okonkwo do whenever he thought of his father's weakness and failure?
2. What did Okonkwo tell himself about his part in Ikemefuna's death?
3. What did Obierika tell Okonkwo about his part in Ikemefuna's death?
4. Describe the meeting to determine Obierika's daughter's bride price.
5. The men began discussing rumors about white men. Who did the men think the white men were?
6. Describe the relationship between Ekwefi and Ezinma.
7. Describe Ekwefi's difficulties in getting pregnant.
8. What did the medicine man tell Okonkwo after the death of Ekwefi's second child?
9. Describe the burial of Ekwefi's third child, and the reason for it.
10. Explain the significance of Ezinma's *iyi-uwa*.
11. How did Okonkwo cure Ezinma's *iba* illness?
12. What was the purpose of the ceremony described in Chapter 10?

Short Answer Study Questions-*Things Fall Apart*, p. 2

Chapters 11-13
1. What did Chielo want with Ezinma?
2. What did Ekwefi do?
3. What did Okonkwo do when Chielo took Ezinma?
4. What was the purpose of the *uri* ceremony?
5. What was the significance in the amount of wine the family brought?
6. What happened at the end of the ceremony?
7. Describe Ezeudu's funeral.
8. How did the author describe a man's life?
9. What happened during the frenzy?
10. What was the result of Okonkwo's action?
11. What was the reason for the clan's actions against Okonkwo?
12. What did Obierika think about after this calamity, and what was his conclusion?

Chapters 14-19
1. Where did Okonkwo take his family to live?
2. How did Okonkwo feel about his circumstances?
3. Why did Uchendu talk to Okonkwo about the Mother Supreme?
4. Who came to visit Okonkwo during the second year of exile, and why?
5. Briefly retell the story of the destruction of Abame.
6. What was Obierika's reaction to the story?
7. What event did Obierika describe on his next visit, two years later?
8. Who had Obierika found among the missionaries?
9. What was the iron horse?
10. Where did the missionaries in Mbanta build their church, why were they given that particular piece of land, and what happened to them?
11. What was it about Nwoye's actions that disturbed Okonkwo so much?
12. What group wanted to be admitted to the Christian church, and what happened?
13. Describe the incident with the sacred python.
14. What did Okonkwo do before he left Mbanta when his exile was ended?
15. What was the one elder's message to those at the feast?

Short Answer Study Questions-*Things Fall Apart*, p. 3

Chapters 20-25
1. How did Okonkwo feel about his return to the clan?
2. What message did Okonkwo give to his sons and daughters after Nwoye left the family?
3. Describe the changes that had come to Umuofia in the seven years that Okonkwo was in exile.
4. Okonkwo asked Obierika why the people had lost their power to fight. What was Obierika's reply?
5. How did many of the other villagers feel about these changes?
6. What was Mr. Brown's conclusion about the religion of the clan? How did he act to gain converts?
7. About what was Okonkwo grieving?
8. Describe the conflict started by Enoch.
9. What was the result of the action taken by the *egwuguw*?
10. How did Okonkwo feel when he returned from the white man's prison?
11. Why did the men meet in the marketplace?
12. What event happened in the marketplace?
13. What happened to Okonkwo?
14. What did Obierika tell the Commissioner?
15. What was the Commissioner's reaction to the incident?

Short Answer Study Questions-*Things Fall Apart*, p. 4

Chapters 1-4

1. Why was Okonkwo famous?
    He was a well known, successful wrestler when he was young. As an adult, he was a wealthy farmer and strong warrior.

2. Describe Unoka.
    He was Okonkwo's father. He was lazy and improvident. He constantly borrowed money that he didn't repay.

3. Why had the men of Umuofia called a meeting?
    The men of Mbaino, a neighboring village, had murdered a woman of Umuofia, and the men wanted revenge.

4. Where does the story take place?
    It takes place in the village of Umuofia, in Africa.

5. What influence did the oracle have on decisions made in Umuofia?
    The men didn't go to war unless the reason was accepted by the oracle.

6. What were Okonkwo's greatest fear and greatest passion?
    He was afraid that he would resemble his father. His greatest passion was to hate everything his father loved.

7. What upset Okonkwo most about his son, Nwoye?
    Nwoye was lazy, not ambitious.

8. What did Okonkwo bring home from his trip to Mbaino?
    He brought home a boy from the village. His name was Ikemefuna.

9. How did Okonkwo begin his prosperous career?
    He took gifts to a wealthy man in the village and asked him for some yam seeds.

10. How did Ikemefuna react to living with Okonkwo's family?
    At fist he tried to run away, and refused to eat. The family treated him well and he began to\ get used to living with them.

11. What unheard of thing did Okonkwo do during the Week of Peace?
    He beat his second wife.

Short Answer Study Questions-*Things Fall Apart*, p. 5

12. How did the people view yams?
    Yams stood for manliness, and one who could feed his family on yams all year was a great man.

<u>Chapters 5-7</u>

1. Describe the Feast of the New Yam.
    The Feast of the New Yam was held yearly before the harvest. It honored the earth goddess, Ani, and the ancestral spirits of the clan. New yams were offered to these powers. The old yams of the previous year were disposed of. All cooking and serving utensils were washed. Yam foo-foo and vegetable soup were the main ceremonial dishes.

2. Who was Okonkwo's favorite child, and what did he often say about the child?
    His favorite child was Ezinma, daughter of Ekwefi. He often said it was a shame she wasn't a boy.

3. What unacceptable thing did Okonkwo do just before the Feast of the New Yam?
    He beat his second wife, Ekwefi, then fired his gun at her.

4. Who was Chielo, and why was she important?
    She was the priestess of Agbala, the Oracle of the Hills and the Caves.

5. What sport did the villagers enjoy watching during their feasting?
    They enjoyed watching the young men of the village wrestle.

6. What influence did Ikemefuna have on Nwoye?
    Ikemefuna acted as an elder brother. He made Nwoye feel grown up. Nwoye began acting more like a man.

7. How did Okonkwo feel about Ikemefuna's influence on Nwoye?
    He was inwardly pleased, although he would not show it. He did, however, invite the boys to sit with him and told them stories of the land.

8. How did the villagers feel about the coming of the locusts, and what did they do about it?
    They were delighted to have the locusts. They caught as many a possible, roasted them, and ate them as a delicacy.

9. What did the village decide to do with Ikemefuna?
    The oracle decided that the villagers should kill him.

Short Answer Study Questions-*Things Fall Apart*, p. 6

10. Who struck the last blow to Ikemefuna, and why?
    Okonkwo did, because he was afraid of being thought weak.

Chapters 8-10
1. What did Okonkwo do whenever he thought of his father's weakness and failure?
   He thought of his own strength and success.

2. What did Okonkwo tell himself about his part in Ikemefuna's death?
   He said he was becoming a woman. A man who had killed five men in battle should not fall to pieces over the death of a boy.

3. What did Obierika tell Okonkwo about his part in Ikemefuna's death?
   Obierika said it was the kind of action that would not please the Earth; that the goddess would wipe out an entire family for such an action.

4. Describe the meeting to determine Obierika's daughter's bride price.
   The suitor, Ibe, his father, Ukegbu, and uncle met with Obierika, his brothers, his son, and Okonkwo. They ate kola nuts and drank palm wine. Then Obierika gave Ukegbu a bundle of thirty short broomsticks. Ukegbu and his clan took the sticks outside. When they returned they gave a bundle of fifteen sticks to Obierika. He added ten more sticks and gave the bundle back. The two groups finally agreed at a bride-price of twenty bags of cowries.

5. The men began discussing rumors about white men. Who did they think the white men were?
   The polite word for leprosy was "the white skin." The men in the hut thought the white men were lepers.

6. Describe the relationship between Ekwefi and Ezinma.
   It was more like the companionship of equals, rather than that of mother and daughter.

7. Describe Ekwefi's difficulties in getting pregnant.
   She had borne ten children, but nine of them had died in infancy. She began giving them names like "Death, I implore you" and "May it not happen again."

8. What did the medicine man tell Okonkwo after the death of Ekwefi's second child?
   He said there was an *ogbanje*, a wicked child who, when it died, re-entered its mother's womb to be born again. He said Ekwefi should go and stay with her people when she became pregnant again.

Short Answer Study Questions-*Things Fall Apart*, p. 7

9. Describe the burial of Ekwefi's third child, and the reason for it.
    The medicine man ordered that there be no mourning or funeral. He mutilated the dead child and buried it in the Evil forest. He said this would make the *ogbanje* think about coming again.

10. Explain the significance of Ezinma's *iyi-uwa*.
    This was a special kind of stone that formed the link between an *ogbanje* and the spirit world. If it were discovered, then the child would not die. When Okagbue found Ezinma's *iyi-uwa*, the people knew Ezinma's troubles were over.

Chapters 8-10 continued

11. How did Okonkwo cure Ezinma's *iba* illness?
    He brewed a potion made of leaves and herbs, then put her over the steam.

12. What was the purpose of the ceremony described in Chapter 10?
    A woman's birth family was having a dispute with her husband because he was mistreating her. The only decision the man would accept in the case was that of the symbolic meeting of the clan spirits.

Chapters 11-13

1. What did Chielo want with Ezinma?
    Chielo wanted to take Ezinma to see Agbala.

2. What did Ekwefi do?
    She followed Chielo and Ezinma to the cave of Agbala.

3. What did Okonkwo do when Chielo took Ezinma?
    He followed her, too, with his machete.

4. What was the purpose of the *uri* ceremony?
    The family of the suitor was bringing palm-wine to Obierika and his extensive group of kinsmen.

5. What was the significance in the amount of wine the family brought?
    They were thought to be behaving like men if they brought a generous amount.

6. What happened at the end of the ceremony?
    The bride-to-be went to live with her suitor's family for seven market weeks.

Short Answer Study Questions-*Things Fall Apart*, p. 8

7. Describe Ezeudu's funeral.
    He was the clan elder, so there was a great ceremony. There was a lot of shouting, drum beating, and firing of guns.

8. How did the author describe a man's life?
    A man's life was a series of transition rites which brought him closer to death and his ancestors.

9. What happened during the frenzy?
    Okonkwo accidentally shot a boy.

10. What was the result of Okonkwo's action?
    He and his family were forced to leave the clan for seven years. The men from Ezeudu's quarter demolished Okonkwo's houses and barn, and killed his animals.

11. What was the reason for the clan's actions against Okonkwo?
    They were cleansing the land which Okonkwo had polluted. It was not revenge.

12. What did Obierika think about after this calamity, and what was his conclusion?
    He wondered why a man should suffer because of an inadvertent mistake. He also wondered why he had to throw away his wife's twins when they were born. He concluded that the clan had to punish offenses so that the Earth would not loose her wrath on all the land, instead of just on the offender.

Chapters 14-19
1. Where did Okonkwo take his family to live?
    He took them to live with his mother's kinsmen in Mbanta.

2. How did Okonkwo feel about his circumstances?
    He thought his personal god or *chi* was not meant for great things. He was feeling despair.

3. Why did Uchendu talk to Okonkwo about the Mother Supreme?
    He wanted Okonkwo to realize that his despair was, comparatively, not that great, and that he owed it to his family to comfort and support them. He told Okonkwo not to refuse comfort in his mother's homeland, or he would displease the dead.

4. Who came to visit Okonkwo during the second year of exile, and why?
    Obierika came to bring Okonkwo news of the village and money from the yam crop he was tending until Okonkwo returned home.

Short Answer Study Questions-*Things Fall Apart*, p. 9

5. Briefly retell the story of the destruction of Abame.
    A white man riding an iron horse had come to the village. The elders killed the man and tied his iron horse to their sacred tree. A few months later, three white men came, saw the iron horse, and left again. A few weeks later, on market day, the white men surrounded the market and killed all of the people there.

6. What was Obierika's reaction to the story?
    He said he was afraid, because he had heard other stories about white men with powerful guns who took men away as slaves.

7. What event did Obierika describe on his next visit, two years later?
    The missionaries had come to Umuofia. They had built a church, won converts, and were sending evangelists to surrounding villages.

8. Who had Obierika found among the missionaries?
    He had found Okonkwo's son, Nwoye.

9. What was the iron horse?
    It was a bicycle.

10. Where did the missionaries in Mbanta build their church, why were they given that particular piece of land, and what happened to them?
    The villagers gave the missionaries land in the Evil Forest, because they didn't really want them, and they thought the missionaries would decline the offer. When the missionaries were alive and well when the villagers expected them to be dead, they won more converts.

11. What was it about Nwoye's actions that disturbed Okonkwo so much?
    He was concerned that Nwoye and his other male children would abandon their ancestors. He pictured himself and his fathers waiting in vain for worship and sacrifice.

12. What group wanted to be admitted to the Christian church, and what happened?
    The osu, or outcasts, wanted to be admitted. Mr. Kiaga agreed, on the condition that they shave their long, tangled hair. They did so, and survived, and became strong proponents of the faith.

Short Answer Study Questions-*Things Fall Apart*, p. 10

13. Describe the incident with the sacred python.
    The sacred python was the most revered animal in the area. It was thought to be the emanation of the god of water. No one had ever even thought of killing it. One of the former outcasts, now a Christian, had alledgedly killed the sacred python, although it was never proved. The elders decided to ostracize the Christians. Soon after this decision, the alleged killer died, and the clan agreed not to bother the other Christians.

14. What did Okonkwo do before he left Mbanta when his exile was ended?
    He held a great feast to thank his mother's kinsmen for their hospitality.

15. What was the one elder's message to those at the feast?
    He told them he feared for their generation because they didn't understand how strong the bonds of kinship should be. He was concerned because they had let this strange religion start to break apart their clans.

Chapters 20-25
1. How did Okonkwo feel about his return to the clan?
   He knew that he had lost a lot of ground, but he was determined to return with a flourish, and regain the lost time.

2. What message did Okonkwo give to his sons and daughters after Nwoye left the family?
   He told his sons if they were going to be weak and follow Nwoye, they should do it while he was alive. If they turned against him after he died, he would return and break their necks. He asked his daughters to wait until they returned to Umuofia to marry.

3. Describe the changes that had come to Umuofia in the seven years that Okonkwo was in exile.
   The Christian church had many converts. The white men had brought a government and built a court. The new prison was full of men who had broken the white men's laws.

4. Okonkwo asked Obierika why the people had lost their power to fight. What was Obierika's reply?
   He said that too many of their people had joined with the white men in their religion and in upholding their laws. The white men managed to divide the clans and they were falling apart.

5. How did many of the other villagers feel about these changes?
   They liked the trading store and the resultant money that was coming into Umuofia. They were also starting to think that the religion had some substance.

Short Answer Study Questions-*Things Fall Apart*, p. 11

6. What was Mr. Brown's conclusion about the religion of the clan? How did he act to gain converts?
    He decided a frontal attack would not work. Instead, he built a school and a hospital. When the people began seeing results from their schooling, and had illnesses healed, they began converting.

7. About what was Okonkwo grieving?
    He mourned for the clan because it was falling apart. He also mourned for the men, because he thought they were getting soft, like women.

8. Describe the conflict started by Enoch.
    Enoch publicly unmasked one of the *egwugwu*, thus killing an ancestral spirit. The rest of the masked *egwugwu* destroyed Enoch's compound, then headed for the church. They destroyed the church, but let Mr. Smith and the others live.

9. What was the result of the action taken by the *egwuguw*?
    Okonkwo and five of the leaders were imprisoned by the District Commissioner. The village of Umuofia was fined 200 bags of cowries.

10. How did Okonkwo feel when he returned from the white man's prison?
    He was full of hate and bitterness, and wanted revenge.

11. Why did the men meet in the marketplace?
    They met to discuss what their course of action should be.

12. What event happened in the marketplace?
    Five court messengers came to stop the meeting. Okonkwo decapitated one of them.

13. What happened to Okonwo?
    He hanged himself.

14. What did Obierika tell the Commissioner?
    Obierika said the Commissioner had driven Okonkwo to kill himself.

15. What was the commissioner's reaction to the incident?
    He thought about how he could use the incident as material in his book.

MULTIPLE CHOICE STUDY QUESTIONS-*Things Fall Apart*

Chapters 1-4

1. Why was Okonkwo famous?
     A. He could throw a spear farther than anyone else in the tribe.
     B. He had the most wives and the most children. This was taken to be a sign of prosperity.
     C. He was a well known, successful wrestler when he was young. As an adult, he was a wealthy farmer and strong warrior.
     D. He was the only man in the village who had traveled more than one hundred miles away from the village.

2. Which of the following statements does **not** describe Unoka?
     A. He was the best drummer in the clan.
     B. He was Okonkwo's father.
     C. He was lazy and improvident.
     D. He constantly borrowed money that he did not repay.

3. True or False: The men in Okonkwo's village had murdered a woman from a neighboring village, and her kinsmen wanted revenge.
     A. True
     B. False

4. What is the setting of the beginning of the story?
     A. It takes place in Idemili.
     B. It takes place in Amalinze.
     C. It takes place in Okoye.
     D. It takes place in Umuofia.

5. What influenced the decisions made in Umuofia?
     A. It was the oracle.
     B. It was the harmattan.
     C. It was the Ibo.
     D. It was the *ogene*.

6. True or false: Okonkwo's greatest fear was that he would resemble his father.
     A. True
     B. False

Multiple Choice Study Questions-*Things Fall Apart*, p. 2.

7. What upset Okonkwo most about his son, Nwoye?
    A. Nwoye looked like Okonkwo's father.
    B. Nwoye was short, and Okonkwo wanted him to be tall.
    C. Nwoye was lazy, not ambitious.
    D. Nwoye was very belligerent.

8. What did Okonkwo bring home from his trip to Mbaino?
    A. He brought home a new strain of yam seeds.
    B. He brought home a boy from the village. His name was Ikemefuna.
    C. He brought home a new wife.
    D. He brought home a disease that rapidly spread through the village.

9. How did Okonkwo begin his prosperous career?
    A. He married the daughter of a rich man and took over his farm.
    B. He stole his father's money and used it for himself.
    C. He saved all of the prize money from his wrestling and used it to buy land.
    D. He took gifts to a wealthy man in the village and asked him for some yam seeds.

10. True or False: Ikemefuna hated living with Okonkwo's family. He had to be tied down to be kept from running away.
    A. True
    B. False

11. What unheard of thing did Okonkwo do during the Week of Peace?
    A. He beat his second wife.
    B. He killed a goat and ate the meat.
    C. He drank wine.
    D. He got into a fight with one of his neighbors.

12. What food stood for manliness, and was a sign of prosperity?
    A. It was potatoes.
    B. It was yams.
    C. It was coconuts.
    D. It was plantains.

Multiple Choice Study Questions-*Things Fall Apart*, p. 3

Chapters 5-7

1. Which of the following does **not** describe the Feast of the New Yam?
    A. The youngest girl in the clan was sacrificed to insure a good crop.
    B. New yams were offered to the earth goddess, Ani, and the ancestral spirits of the clan.
    C. The old yams of the previous year were disposed of.
    D. All cooking and serving utensils were washed.

2. What did Okonkwo often say about Ezinma?
    A. He said she looked just like her mother, who was his favorite wife.
    B. He said she should bring a good bride-price, and marry a rich man.
    C. He said it was a shame she wasn't a boy.
    D. He said she was a spirit-being come to life.

3. What unacceptable thing did Okonkwo do just before the Feast of the New Yam?
    A. He got drunk in public.
    B. He beat his second wife, Ekwefi, then fired his gun at her.
    C. He planted his new crop of yam seeds before the proper ceremonies were held.
    D. He ate yams. It was forbidden to do this for a week before the festival.

4. Who was Chielo, and why was she important?
    A. She was the priestess of Agbala, the Oracle of the Hills and the Caves.
    B. She was Okonkwo's mother, who was revered as the elder in the clan.
    C. She was the first wife of the man with the most titles in the clan, and had power over her husband's decisions.
    D. She was the village matchmaker. Everyone wanted to be on her good side so that she would find good spouses for their children.

5. What sport did the villages enjoy watching during their feasting?
    A. They enjoyed watching the young men of the village play soccer.
    B. They enjoyed watching the young men of the village run foot-races.
    C. They enjoyed watching the young men of the village climb the palm trees.
    D. They enjoyed watching the young men of the village wrestle.

6. True or False: Ikemefuna was a bad influence on Nwoye. He taught Nwoye to be defiant and rebellious.
    A. True
    B. False

Multiple Choice Study Questions-*Things Fall Apart*, p. 4

7. How did Okonkwo feel about Ikemefuna's influence on Nwoye?
    A. He was inwardly pleased, although he would not show it.
    B. He was displeased, and ignored the two boys.

8. What did the villagers do when the locusts came?
    A. They blockaded themselves in their huts until the locusts had gone.
    B. They set fire to the fields to drive the locusts away.
    C. They ran away to a neighboring village.
    D. They caught as many as possible, roasted them, and ate them as a delicacy.

9. How did the villagers decide to kill Ikemefuna?
    A. They read palm leaves and interpreted them.
    B. They took a vote.
    C. They asked the oracle.
    D. They gave him a choice between death and life-long slavery. He chose death.

10. Who struck the last blow to Ikemefuna, and why?
    A. Nwoye did, to please his father.
    B. Okonkwo did, because he was afraid of being thought weak.
    C. Ogbuefi Ezeudu did, because he was the oldest man in the village.
    D. Obierika did, because he didn't like Ikemefuna.

Multiple Choice Study Questions-*Things Fall Apart*, p. 5

Chapters 8-10

1. What did Okonkwo do whenever he thought of his father's weakness and failure?
    A. He beat a few of his children.
    B. He got drunk for a few days.
    C. He thought of his own strength and success.
    D. He prayed to his ancestral gods for strength.

2. What did Okonkwo tell himself about his part in Ikemefuna's death?
    A. He was proud of himself. He thought it increased his prestige in the clan.
    B. He told himself the boy didn't matter, since he was not from the clan.
    C. He knew he was wrong, and promised to make it up to the boy's spirit by making offerings to the Oracle.
    D. He said he was becoming a woman. A man who had killed five men in battle should not fall to pieces over the death of a boy.

3. True or False: Obierika said Okonkwo's action was the kind of action that would not please the Earth; that the goddess would wipe out an entire family for such an action.
    A. True
    B. False

4. What did Ibe and his relatives use to determine a bride price for Obierika's daughter?
    A. They held a wrestling match. The winner determined the price.
    B. They used a bundle of sticks.
    C. They used kola nuts.
    D. They used pots of palm wine.

5. The men began discussing rumors about white men. Who did the men think the white men were?
    A. They thought the men were spirits.
    B. They thought the men were spies from a neighboring village.
    C. They thought the men were lepers.
    D. They thought the men were travelers from another part of Africa.

6. True or False: Ekwefi was jealous of the attention that Okonkwo paid to their daughter, Ezinma.
    A. True
    B. False

Multiple Choice Study Questions-*Things Fall Apart*, p. 6

7. True or False: Ekwefi had borne ten children, but nine of them had died in infancy. She began giving them names like "Death, I implore you," and "May it not happen again."
    A. True
    B. False

8. True or False: An *ogbanje* was a wicked child who, when it died, re-entered its mother's womb to be born again.
    A. True
    B. False

9. What did the medicine man do to Ekwefi's third child when it died?
    A. He performed a special ceremony that was supposed to make it become good.
    B. He took it to his own hut and mummified it. That way he could guard it and make sure it would not bother Ekwefi again.
    C. He buried it with a lot of good food and a bag of cowries, so that it would be happy and not return.
    D. He mutilated the dead child and buried it in the Evil Forest. He said this would make the *ogbange* think about coming again.

10. What was Ezinma's *iyi-uwa*, or link with the *ogbanje*?
    A. It was a birth-mark, like a mole, that had to be removed.
    B. It was a special kind of stone that was buried in the ground.
    C. It was a yam seed that was square in shape.
    D. It was a cowry shell that was a different color than the rest.

11. How did Okonkwo cure Ezinma's *iba* illness?
    A. He used a voodoo doll.
    B. He made sacrifices of his best yams to the oracle.
    C. He brewed a potion made of leaves and herbs, then put her over the steam.
    D. He sent for the medicine man in the next village.

12. What was the purpose of the ceremony described in Chapter 10?
    A. A woman's birth family was having a dispute with her husband because he was mistreating her. The clan spirits would decide the outcome.
    B. It was to determine how much land to give the man and his new wife.
    C. It was a fertility right to insure that the couple had many healthy children.
    D. It was an annual play put on by the elders to remind the men and women how they should treat each other.

Multiple Choice Study Questions-*Things Fall Apart*, p. 7

Chapters 11-13
1. Who wanted to take Ezinma to see Agbala?
    A. Obierika did.
    B. Chielo did.
    C. Nwoye did.
    D. The other wives did.

2. What did Ekwefi do?
    A. She stayed home and made sacrifices at her personal altar.
    B. She got hysterical and had to be tied down by the other wives.
    C. She followed them to the cave of Agbala.
    D. She went to sleep, because she was not worried.

3. What did Okonkwo do?
    A. He carried Ezinma.
    B. He got drunk.
    C. He followed them with his machete.
    D. He roused the other men to follow after Ezinma and her guardian.

4. Who were the central figures in the *uri* ceremony?
    A. It was the bride and her mother.
    B. It was the groom and his mother.
    C. It was the bride and groom.
    D. It was the fathers of the bride and groom.

5. The groom's family were thought to be behaving like men if they brought a generous amount of what item?
    A. It was yam seeds.
    B. It was palm-wine.
    C. It was kola nuts.
    D. It was cowry shells.

6. What happened at the end of the ceremony?
    A. The bride-to-be went to live with her suitor's family for seven market weeks.
    B. The couple was given land and a hut to live in.
    C. The groom moved in with the bride and her family.
    D. The bride and groom traded families for a week.

Multiple Choice Study Questions-*Things Fall Apart*, p. 8

7. Which did **not** happen during Ezeudu's funeral?
    A. There was a lot of shouting.
    B. There was a lot of drum beating.
    C. The men and boys had wrestling matches.
    D. The men fired their guns.

8. True or False: The author describes a man's life as a continual struggle to get away from his ancestors.
    A. True
    B. False

9. How did Okonkwo kill the boy?
    A. He choked him to death on purpose.
    B. He accidentally killed him with his machete.
    C. He deliberately poisoned the boy.
    D. He accidentally shot him.

10. What was the result of Okonkwo's action?
    A. He had to give two of his sons to the boy's family.
    B. He had to pay the boy's family half of his wealth.
    C. He and his family were forced to leave the clan for seven years.
    D. He was sent into the Evil Forest to live for one week. If he survived, he was allowed to return to the clan.

11. Why did the men from Ezeudu's quarter demolish Okonkwo's houses and barn, and kill his animals?
    A. They were cleansing the land which Okonkwo had polluted.
    B. They were drunk and were seeking revenge.
    C. The oracle told them to do it.
    D. They were permitted by law to do anything they wanted short of killing Okonkwo and his family.

12. One person wondered why a man should suffer because of an inadvertent mistake. He/she also wondered why twins had to be thrown away. This person concluded that the clan had to punish offenses so that the Earth would not loose her wrath on all the land. Who was it?
    A. It was Ezinma.
    B. It was Chielo.
    C. It was Obierika.
    D. It was Nwoye.

Multiple Choice Study Questions-*Things Fall Apart*, p. 9

Chapters 14-19

1. Where did Okonkwo take his family to live?
    A. He took them to live with his father's people.
    B. He took them to live with his mother's kinsmen.
    C. He sent all of his wives back to their own villages and went to live with a friend.
    D. He took them to live in the wilderness between his village and the next.

2. True or False: Okonkwo thought his personal god or *chi* was not meant for great things. He was feeling despair.
    A. True
    B. False

3. Uchendu talked to Okonkwo about the Mother Supreme. Which of the following was **not** one of the points he made?
    A. He wanted Okonkwo to realize that his despair, comparatively, was not that great.
    B. He said Okonkwo owed it to his family to comfort and support them.
    C. He said this was Okonkwo's chance to start over where no one would compare him to to his father.
    D. He told Okonkwo not to refuse comfort in his mother's homeland, or he would displease the dead.

4. Who came to visit Okonkwo during the second year of exile, and why?
    A. Chielo came to bless them and check on Ezinma's health.
    B. Ojiugo's parents came to bring them gifts.
    C. Obierika came to bring Okonkwo news of the village and money from the yam crop he was tending until Okonkwo returned home.
    D. Ezeudu's clansmen came to make sure Okonkwo was still in exile.

5. Why was the village of Abame destroyed?
    A. The elders killed a white man who had come into the town, and other white men destroyed the village in retribution.
    B. The other villages were jealous of their wealth, so they killed the people and stole the money and property.
    C. There had been a bad outbreak of *iba*. The village elders decided the town had to be burned down in order to save the surrounding villages.
    D. There had been an uprising between two families. It got out of hand, and they destroyed each other and everyone else in the process.

Multiple Choice Study Questions-*Things Fall Apart*, p. 10

6. What was Obierika's reaction to the story?
   A. He didn't believe it at all. He said it was nonsense dreamed up by women.
   B. He said he was afraid, because he had heard other such stories.

7. True or False: On his next visit two years later, Obierika said the missionaries had come to Umuofia.
   A. True
   B. False

8. Who had Obierika found among the missionaries?
   A. He had found his son, Maduka.
   B. He had found Uchendu.
   C. He had found Okonkwo's son, Nwoye.
   D. He had found his youngest wife and her children.

9. What was the iron horse?
   A. It was the new railroad that the whites were building with slave labor.
   B. It was an automobile.
   C. It was a walking stick made of aluminum.
   D. It was a bicycle.

10. True or False: The villagers gave the missionaries a piece of the best land in the village because it was their custom to be polite to newcomers.
    A. True
    B. False

11. True or False: Okonkwo was concerned that Nwoye and his other male children would abandon their ancestors. He pictured himself and his fathers waiting in vain for worship and sacrifice.
    A. True
    B. False

12. What group was admitted to the Christian church and became strong followers?
    A. It was the women and children.
    B. It was the *egwugwu*.
    C. It was the *osu*.
    D. It was the *efulefu*.

Multiple Choice Study Questions-*Things Fall Apart*, p. 11

13. What sacred animal was allegedly killed by one of the newly converted Christians?
    A. It was the goat.
    B. It was the cow.
    C. It was the chicken.
    D. It was the python.

14. What did Okonkwo do before he left Mbanta when his exile was ended?
    A. He gave all of his belongings to his mother's family.
    B. He held a great feast to thank his mother's kinsmen for their hospitality.
    C. He burned down his compound.
    D. He went to pray at his mother's grave.

15. True or False: One of the elders told the younger clan members he feared for their generation because they didn't understand how strong the bonds of kinship should be. He was concerned because they had let this strange religion start to break apart their clans.
    A. True
    B. False

Multiple Choice Study Questions-*Things Fall Apart*, p. 12

Chapters 20-25

1. How did Okonkwo feel about his return to the clan?
    A. He was angry at them for sending him away, and wanted revenge.
    B. He knew that he had lost a lot of ground, but he was determined to return with a flourish, and retain the lost time.
    C. He was ashamed of what he had done, and just wanted to be left alone.
    D. He realized that he preferred living with his mother's people.

2. Which of the following was **not** one of the messages Okonkwo gave to his sons and daughters after Nwoye left the family?
    A. If his were going to be weak and follow Nwoye, they should do it while he was alive.
    B. If they turned against him after he died, he would return and break their necks.
    C. He asked his daughters to wait until they returned to Umuofia to marry.
    D. He asked all of his children to name their firstborn after him.

3. Which of the following was **not** one of the changes that had come to Umuofia in the seven years that Okonkwo was inexile?
    A. The Christian church had many converts.
    B. The white men had brought a government and built a court.
    C. The villages had to pay taxes to the white men.
    D. The new prison was full of men who had broken the white men's law.

4. Okonkwo asked Obierika why the people had lost their power to fight. What was Obierika's reply?
    A. He said the chi of the villages was worn out.
    B. The white man managed to divide the clans and they were falling apart.
    C. He said the white man's God was stronger than their Chukwu.
    D. He said the white men had put an evil spell on the villages.

5. True or False: Many of the other villagers liked the trading store and the resultant money that was coming into Umuofia. They were also starting to think that the religion had some substance.
    A. True
    B. False

6. How did Mr. Brown act to gain converts?
    A. He used a frontal attack.
    B. He threatened to kill all of the children if the adults did not convert.
    C. He bribed them with money.
    D. He built a school and a hospital.

Multiple Choice Study Questions-*Things Fall Apart*, p. 13

Chapters 20-25 continued

7. True or False: Okonkwo was grieving mostly because he never got the opportunity to regain his former status.
    A. True
    B. False

8. What did Enoch do?
    A. He killed the sacred python.
    B. Enoch publicly unmasked one of the *egwugwu*, thus killing an ancestral spirit.
    C. He molested one of the young girls.
    D. He stole food from some of the women.

9. What did the clan members do in retaliation?
    A. They killed Enoch.
    B. They killed Mr. Smith and the Christians.
    C. They destroyed the church and Enoch's compound.
    D. They drove the Christians out of the village.

10. What was the result of the action taken by the *egwuguw*?
    A. Okonkwo and five of the leaders were imprisoned. The village of Umuofia was fined 200 bags of cowries.
    B. The village was destroyed by the government's army.
    C. Mr. Smith became ill and returned to England.
    D. They were all hanged.

11. What event happened in the marketplace?
    A. The men of the village opened fire on the messengers and killed them all.
    B. Five court messengers came to stop the meeting. Okonkwo decapitated one of them.
    C. The men of the village turned it over to the white men.
    D. The men decided to contact the other villages and make plans for war.

12. What happened to Okonkwo?
    A. He hanged himself.
    B. He was taken prisoner.
    C. He escaped into the forest.
    D. He finally accepted the white man's rule.

MULTIPLE CHOICE STUDY QUESTIONS ANSWER KEY - *Things Fall Apart*

Chapter 1-4
1. C
2. A
3. B
4. D
5. A
6. A True
7. C
8. B
9. D
10. B False
11. A
12. B

Chapters 5-7
1. A
2. C
3. B
4. A
5. D
6. B False
7. A
8. D
9. C
10. B

Chapters 8-10
1. C
2. D
3. A True
4. B
5. C
6. B False
7. A
8. A True
9. D
10. B
11. C
12. A

Chapters 11-13
1. B
2. C
3. C
4. A
5. B
6. A
7. C
8. B
9. D
10. C
11. A
12. C

Chapters 14-19
1. B
2. A True
3. C
4. C
5. A
6. B
7. A True
8. C
9. D
10. B False
11. A True
12. C
13. D
14. B
15. A True

Chapters 20-25
1. B
2. D
3. C
4. B
5. A True
6. D
7. B False
8. B
9. C
10. A
11. B
12. A

PREREADING VOCABULARY WORKSHEETS

PREREADING VOCABULARY WORKSHEETS-*Things Fall Apart*

<u>Chapters 1-4</u>

Part I: Using Prior Knowledge and Context Clues
Below are the sentences in which the vocabulary words appear in the text. Read the sentence.
Use any clues you can find in the sentence combined with your prior knowledge, and write what you think the underlined words mean in the space provided.

1. The drums beat and the flutes sang and the *spectators* held their breath.

2. In his day he was lazy and *improvident* and was quite incapable of thinking about tomorrow.

3. He wore a *haggard* and mournful look except when he was drinking or playing his flute.

4. An ultimatum was immediately dispatched to Mbaino asking them to choose between war on the one hand, and on the other the offer of a young man and a virgin as *compensation*.

5.& 6. And so when Okonkwo of Umuofia arrived at Mbaino as the proud and *imperious emissary* of war, he was treated with great honor and respect, and two days later he returned home with a lad of fifteen and a young virgin.

7. His wives, especially the youngest, lived in *perpetual* fear of his fiery temper, and so did his little children.

8. It was deeper and more intimate than the fear of evil and *capricious* gods and of magic, the fear of the forest, and of the forces of nature, red in tooth and claw.

9. Okonkwo's first son, Nwoye, was then twelve years old but was already causing his father great anxiety for his *incipient* laziness.

10. But he was struck, as most people were, by Okonkwo's *brusqueness* in dealing with less successful men.

11. Only a week ago a man had contradicted him at a *kindred* meeting which they held to discuss the next ancestral feast.

12. But it was really not true that Okonkwo's palm kernels had been cracked for him by a *benevolent* spirit.

Prereading Vocabulary Worksheets-*Things Fall Apart*, p. 2

Note: The *harmattan* is a dry, dusty wind that blows from the Sahara and along the northwestern coast of Africa.

Part II: Determining the Meaning   Match the vocabulary words to their dictionary definitions.

____ 1. spectators
____ 2. improvident
____ 3. haggard
____ 4. compensation
____ 5. imperious
____ 6. emissary
____ 7. perpetual
____ 8. capricious
____ 9. incipient
____ 10. brusqueness
____ 11. kindred
____ 12. benevolent

A. not providing for the future
B. lasting for eternity
C. characterized by doing good
D. an agent sent in advance
E. observers
F. related to a clan or tribe
G. impulsive and unpredictable
H. abrupt and curt manner; blunt
I. arrogantly domineering; overbearing
J. beginning to exist or appear
K. payment; reimbursement
L. appearing worn and exhausted

Prereading Vocabulary Worksheets-*Things Fall Apart*, p. 3

Chapters 5-7
Part I: Using Prior Knowledge and Context Clues
Below are the sentences in which the vocabulary words appear in the text. Read the sentence. Use any clues you can find in the sentence combined with your prior knowledge, and write what you think the underlined words mean in the space provided.

1. The new year must begin with tasty, fresh yams and not the shriveled and *fibrous* crop of the previous year.

2. All cooking pots, *calabashes*, and wooden bowls were thoroughly washed, especially the wooden mortar in which yam was pounded.

3. The drums rose to a *frenzy*.

4. Old men nodded to the beat of the drums and remembered the days when they wrestled to its *intoxicating* rhythm.

5. Within a short time the two *bouts* were over.

6. Nwoye would *feign* annoyance and grumble aloud about women and their troubles.

7. And when he did this he saw that his father was pleased, and no longer *rebuked* him.

8. They went back to their caves in a distant land, where they were guarded by a race of *stunted* men.

9. They were the *harbingers* sent to survey the land.

10. Okonkwo sat in his obi crunching happily with Ikemefuna and Nwoye, and drinking palm-wine *copiously*....

Prereading Vocabulary Worksheets-*Things Fall Apart*, p. 4

Part II: Determining the Meaning   Match the vocabulary words to their dictionary definitions.

____ 1. fibrous		A.	forerunners
____ 2. calabashes		B.	criticized; reprimanded
____ 3. frenzy		C.	contests; matches
____ 4. intoxicating		D.	violent mental agitation; wild excitement
____ 5. bouts		E.	threadlike
____ 6. feign		F.	abundantly
____ 7. rebuked		G.	stopped from growing
____ 8. stunted		H.	pretend; represent falsely
____ 9. harbingers		I.	stimulating or exciting
____10. copiously		J.	containers made from dried gourds

Prereading Vocabulary Worksheets-*Things Fall Apart*, p. 5

Chapters 8-10
Part I: Using Prior Knowledge and Context Clues
Below are the sentences in which the vocabulary words appear in the text. Read the sentence. Use any clues you can find in the sentence combined with your prior knowledge, and write what you think the underlined words mean in the space provided.

1. "When did you become a shivering old woman," Okonkwo asked himself, "you who are known in all the nine villages for your *valor* in war?"

2. As she buried one child after another her sorrow gave way to despair and then to grim *resignation*.

3. In that way she will *elude* her wicked tormentor and break its evil cycle of birth and death.

4. He brought out a sharp razor from the goatskin bag slung from his left shoulder and began to *mutilate* the child.

5. Her husband's wife took this for *malevolence*, as her husband's wives were wont to do.

6. At first Ekwefi accepted her, as she had the others - with *listless* resignation.

7. ...she could not ignore the fact that some really evil children sometimes misled people into digging up a *specious* one.

8. "No," said Ezinma, whose feeling of importance was manifest in her *sprightly* walk.

9. Most *communal* ceremonies took place at that time of day....

10. The *egwugwu* house was now a *pandemonium* of quavering voices.

11. ...the spirits of the ancestors, just emerged from the earth, greeted themselves in their *esoteric* language.

12. There was a loud murmur of *approbation* from the crowd.

Prereading Vocabulary Worksheets-*Things Fall Apart*, p. 6

Note: The following words are necessary for understanding the story, but will not be tested.

*On the third day he asked his second wife, Ekwefi, to roast *plantains* for him.
   A banana-like fruit, used as a staple food in tropical regions.

*Obierika was sitting outside under the shade of an orange tree making *thatches* from the leaves of the raffia-palm.
   Plant stalks or foliage, such as reeds or palm fronds, used for roofing.

*In Abame and Aninta the title is worth less than two *cowries.*
   Any of various tropical marine gastropods of the family Cypraeidae, having glossy, often brightly marked shells, some of which are used as currency in the South Pacific and Africa.

Part II: Determining the Meaning   Match the vocabulary words to their dictionary definitions.

____ 1. valor
____ 2. resignation
____ 3. elude
____ 4. mutilate
____ 5. malevolence
____ 6. listless
____ 7. specious
____ 8. manifest
____ 9. communal
____ 10. pandemonium
____ 11. esoteric
____ 12. approbation

A. lacking in spirit or energy
B. wild uproar or noise
C. courage in battle; bravery
D. understandable; clear
E. approval
F. evil or harmful influence
G. known only to the chosen few
H. to disfigure or cripple
I. of a group of people.
J. avoid; evade
K. seemingly reliable but incorrect
L. lack of resistance; patient submission

Prereading Vocabulary Worksheets-*Things Fall Apart*, p.9

Chapters 11-13
Part I: Using Prior Knowledge and Context Clues
Below are the sentences in which the vocabulary words appear in the text. Read the sentence. Use any clues you can find in the sentence combined with your prior knowledge, and write what you think the underlined words mean in the space provided.

1. The night was *impenetrably* dark.

2. Nwayieke lived four compounds away, and she was *notorious* for her late cooking.

3. Nothing that happened in the world of animals ever escaped his notice; he was full of *cunning*.

4. His speech was so *eloquent* that all the birds were glad they brought him, and nodded their heads in approval of all he said.

5. After kola nuts had been presented and eaten, the people of the sky set before their guests the most *delectable* dishes Tortoise had ever seen or dreamed of.

6. But Ekwefi did not hear these *consolations*.

7. She hit her left foot against an outcropped root, and terror seized her. It was an ill *omen*.

8. Fireflies went about with their tiny green lamps, which only made the darkness more *profound*.

9. She remembered that night, long ago, when she had seen *Ogbu-agali-odu*, one of those evil *essences* loose upon the world by the potent "medicines" which the tribe had made....

10. The priestess's voice came at longer *intervals* now, but its vigor was undiminished.

11. Ekwefi could now *discern* the figure of the priestess and her burden.

12. It was only on his fourth trip that he had found Ekwefi, and by then he had become *gravely* worried.

Prereading Vocabulary Worksheets-*Things Fall Apart*, p. 9

Part II: Determining the Meaning   Match the vocabulary words to their dictionary definitions.

____ 1. impenetrably
____ 2. notorious
____ 3. cunning
____ 4. eloquent
____ 5. delectable
____ 6. consolations
____ 7. omen
____ 8. profound
____ 9. essences
____ 10. intervals
____ 11. discern
____ 12. gravely

A. not able to be entered or pierced
B. delightful; delicious
C. spiritual or incorporeal entities
D. known widely and usually unfavorably
E. words of comfort
F. time between two specified instants
G. skill in deception
H. prophetic sign
I. distinguish; perceive
J. expressive; persuasive
K. deep; complete
L. serious

Prereading Vocabulary Worksheets - *Things Fall Apart*

<u>Chapters 14-19</u>
Part I: Using Prior Knowledge and Context Clues
Below are the sentences in which the vocabulary words appear in the text. Read the sentence. Use any clues you can find in the sentence combined with your prior knowledge, and write what you think the underlined words mean in the space provided.

1. And he arranged the *requisite* rites and sacrifices.

2. A vague scent of life and green vegetation was *diffused* in the air.

3. He laughed a *mirthless* laughter.

4. Do you know how many children I have buried--children I *begot* in my youth and strength?

5. There is something *ominous* behind the silence.

6. When this was interpreted to the men of Mbanta they broke into *derisive* laughter.

7. Nwoye's *callow* mind was greatly puzzled.

8. Her husband and his family were already becoming highly critical of such a woman and were not unduly *perturbed* when they found she had fled to joint the Christians.

9. & 10. A sudden fury rose within him and he felt a strong desire to take up his machete, go to the church and wipe out the entire *vile* and *miscreant* gang.

11. It was, in fact, one of the men who, in his zeal, brought the church into serious conflict with the clan a year later by killing the sacred python, the *emanation* of the god of water.

12. But let us *ostracize* these men.

Prereading Vocabulary Worksheets-*Things Fall Apart*, p. 12

Part II: Determining the Meaning   Match the vocabulary words to their dictionary definitions.

____ 1. requisite
____ 2. diffused
____ 3. mirthless
____ 4. begot
____ 5. ominous
____ 6. derisive
____ 7. callow
____ 8. perturbed
____ 9. vile
____ 10. miscreant
____ 11. emanate
____ 12. ostracize

A. ridiculing
B. spread in all directions
C. wretch; villain
D. exclude from public favor
E. greatly disturbed
F. without laughter
G. issuing forth
H. threatening
I. youthful; immature
J. loathsome; disgusting
K. produced; fathered
L. necessary requirement

Prereading Vocabulary Worksheets-*Things Fall Apart*, p. 13

Chapters 20-25
Part I: Using Prior Knowledge and Context Clues
Below are the sentences in which the vocabulary words appear in the text. Read the sentence. Use any clues you can find in the sentence combined with your prior knowledge, and write what you think the underlined words mean in the space provided.

1. He would return with a *flourish* and regain the seven wasted years.

2. But it was a *resilient* spirit, and in the end Okonkwo overcame his sorrow.

3. This growing feeling was due to Mr. Brown, the white missionary, who was very firm in restraining his flock from *provoking* the wrath of the clan.

4. Mr. Brown's mission grew from strength to strength, and because of its link with the new administration it earned a new social *prestige*.

5. & 6. He condemned openly Mr. Brown's policy of *compromise* and *accommodation.*

7. Enoch himself was greatly disappointed when he heard this, for he had hoped that a holy war was *imminent.*

8. *Discordant* bells clanged, machetes clashed and the air was full of dust and weird sounds.

9. For a brief moment the onrush of the *egwugwu* was checked by the unexpected *composure* of the two men.

10. Then an unmistakable voice rose above the *tumult* and there was immediate silence.

11. His voice was unmistakable and so he was able to bring immediate peace to the *agitated* spirits.

12. It has bred untold *abominations* and we have come to put an end to it.

Prereading Vocabulary Worksheets-*Things Fall Apart*, p. 14

Part II: Determining the Meaning: Match the vocabulary words to their dictionary definitions.

____ 1. flourish
____ 2. resilient
____ 3. provoking
____ 4. prestige
____ 5. compromise
____ 6. accommodation
____ 7. imminent
____ 8. discordant
____ 9. composure
____ 10. tumult
____ 11. agitated
____ 12. abominations

A. stirred up; disturbed
B. mental calmness
C. help; adaptation
D. angering; causing retaliation
E. something detestable
F. impending; near at hand
G. grow well; prosper
H. adjustment
I. commotion; riot
J. elastic; able to spring back
K. inharmonious; conflicting
L. impression produced by achievement

ANSWER KEY: VOCABULARY WORKSHEETS - *Things Fall Apart*

Chapters 1-4

1. E
2. A
3. L
4. K
5. I
6. D
7. B
8. G
9. J
10. H
11. F
12. C

Chapters 5-7

1. E
2. J
3. D
4. I
5. C
6. H
7. B
8. G
9. A
10. F

Chapters 8-10

1. C
2. L
3. J
4. H
5. F
6. A
7. K
8. D
9. I
10. B
11. G
12. E

Chapters 11-13

1. A
2. D
3. G
4. J
5. B
6. E
7. H
8. K
9. C
10. F
11. I
12. L

Chapters 14-19

1. L
2. B
3. F
4. K
5. B
6. A
7. I
8. E
9. J
10. C
11. G
12. D

Chapters 20-25

1. G
2. J
3. D
4. L
5. H
6. C
7. F
8. K
9. B
10. I
11. A
12. E

DAILY LESSON PLANS

LESSON ONE

Objectives
1. To introduce the *Things Fall Apart* unit
2. To relate students' prior knowledge to the new material
3. To distribute books and other related materials (study Guides, reading assignments)
4. To do the prereading work for the Introduction, Preface, and Letters

Activity #1

Show a map of Africa, focusing on the Niger River area. Have some pictures of the area and the tribes the way they were before England began colonizing the area, and some of modern Nigeria. Explain that this is the setting of the novel. Ask what students think the title could be referring to. Do a group KWL sheet with the students (form included.) Put any information the students know in the K column (What I Know.) Ask students what they want to find out and put that information in the W column (What I want to find out.) Keep the sheet and refer back to it after reading the novel, and complete the L column (What I learned.)

Activity #2

Distribute the materials students will use in this unit. Explain in detail how students are to use these materials.

Study Guides Students should preview the study guide questions before each reading assignment to get a feeling for what events and ideas are important in that section. After reading the section, students will (as a class or individually) answer the questions to review the important events and ideas from that section of the book. Students should keep the study guides as study materials for the unit test.

Reading Assignment Sheet You need to fill in the reading assignment sheet to let students know when their reading has to be completed. You can either write the assignment sheet on a side blackboard or bulletin board and leave it there for students to see each day, or you can "ditto" copies for each student to have. In either case, you should advise students to become very familiar with the reading assignments so they know what is expected of them.

Extra Activities Center The unit resource portion of this unit contains suggestions for a library of related books and articles in your classroom as well as crossword and word search puzzles. Make an extra activities center in your room where you will keep these materials for students to use. (Bring the books and articles in from the library and keep several copies of the puzzles on hand.) Explain to students that these materials are available for students to use when they finish reading assignment or other class work early.

Books Each school has its own rules and regulations regarding student use of school books. Advise students of the procedures that are normal for your school.

Activity #3

Give students some background about the pre-British life of the African tribal clans, especially in Nigeria. Focus on the way of life before and after the colonization of the aea. Provide information about current affairs in Nigeria.

Activity #4

Show students how to preview the study questions and do the vocabulary work for Chapters 1-4 of *Things Fall Apart*. If students do not finish this assignment in class, they should complete it prior to the next class meeting.

LESSON ONE
KWL *Things Fall Apart*

Directions: Before reading, think about what you already know about Chinua Achebe and/or *Things Fall Apart*. Write the information in the K column. Think about what you would like to find out from reading the book. Write your questions in the W column. After you have read the book, use the L column to write the answers to your questions from the W column, and anything else you remember from the book.

K	W	L

LESSON TWO

Objectives
1. To read Chapters 1-4
2. To review the main ideas and events from Chapters 1-4
3. To introduce the Nonfiction Assignments

Activity #1
You may want to read Chapter 1 aloud to the students to set the mood for the novel. Invite willing students to read Chapters 2-4 aloud to the rest of the class.

Activity #2
Give the students time to answer the study guide questions, and then discuss the answers in detail. Write the answers on the board or overhead projector so students can have the correct answers for study purposes. Encourage students to take notes. If the students own their books, encourage them to use high lighter pens to mark important passages and the answers to the study guide questions.

Note: It is a good practice in public speaking and leadership skills for individual students to take charge of leading the discussion of the study questions. Perhaps a different student could go to the front of the class and lead the discussion each day that the study questions are discussed during this unit. Of course, the teacher should guide the discussion when appropriate and be sure to fill in any gaps the students leave.

Activity #3
Distribute copies of the Nonfiction Assignment sheet and go over it in detail with the students. Give them the due date for the assignment (Lesson 14.) Encourage them to focus on topics that are relevant to the novel. Some possible topics are: the colonization methods and policies of Great Britain; a study of one of the tribes in Nigeria, or in another part of Africa; the development of apartheid in South Africa; a comparison and contrast of Christianity and one of the African tribal religions; Nigeria's fight for independence from Great Britain; the conditions in present-day Nigeria.

NONFICTION ASSIGNMENT SHEET - *Things Fall Apart*

(To be completed after reading the required nonfiction article)

Name_____Date_____Class_____

Title of Nonfiction Read_____

Written By_____Publication Date_____

  I. Factual Summary: Write a short summary of the piece you read.

  II. Vocabulary:
    1. With which vocabulary words in the piece did you encounter some degree of difficulty?

    2. How did you resolve your lack of understanding of these words?

  III. Interpretation: What was the main point the author wanted you to get from reading his/her work?

  IV. Criticism:
    1. With which points of the piece did you agree or find easy to accept? Why?

    2. With which points of the piece did you disagree or find difficult to believe? Why?

  V. Personal Response: What do you think about this piece? OR How does this piece influence your ideas?

LESSON THREE

Objectives
1. To do the prereading and vocabulary work for Chapters 5-7
2. To read Chapters 5-7
3. To give students practice reading orally
4. To evaluate students' oral reading

Activity #1
Give students about fifteen minutes to preview the study questions for Chapters 5-7 and do the related vocabulary work.

Activity #2
Have students read Chapters 5-7 of *Things Fall Apart* out loud in class. You probably know the best way to get readers with your class; pick students at random, ask for volunteers, or use whatever method works best for your group. If you have not yet completed an oral reading evaluation for your students for this marking period, this would be a good opportunity to do so. A form is included with this unit for your convenience. If students do not complete reading Chapters 5-7 in class, they should do so prior to your next class meeting.

LESSON FOUR

Objectives
1. To check students' understanding of the main ideas and events from Chapters 1-7
2. To preview the study questions for Chapter 8-10
3. To familiarize students with the vocabulary in Chapters 8-10
4. To read Chapters 8-10

Activity #1
Quiz---distribute quizzes (multiple choice study questions for Chapters 1-4 and/or 5-7) and give students about ten minutes to complete them. Have students exchange papers. Grade the quizzes as a class. Collect the papers for recording the grades.

Activity #2
Give students about fifteen minutes to preview the study questions for Chapters 8-10 and do the related vocabulary work.

Activity#3
Have students read Chapters 8-10 for the rest of the period. If you have not completed the oral reading evaluations, do so now. If the evaluations have been completed, you may want the students to read silently. If students do not complete the reading assignment in class, they should do so prior to your next class meeting.

ORAL READING EVALUATION - *Things Fall Apart*

Name_____Class_____Date_____

SKILL	EXCELLENT	GOOD	AVERAGE	FAIR	POOR
Fluency	5	4	3	2	1
Clarity	5	4	3	2	1
Audibility	5	4	3	2	1
Pronunciation	5	4	3	2	1
_____	5	4	3	2	1
_____	5	4	3	2	1

Total_____Grade_____

Comments:

LESSON FIVE

Objective
1. To give students the opportunity to practice writing to persuade
2. To give the teacher the opportunity to evaluate each student's writing skills

Activity #1
Distribute Writing Assignment #1 and discuss the directions in detail. Allow the remaining class time for students to work on the assignment. Give students an additional two or three days to complete the assignment, if necessary.

Activity #2
Distribute copies of the Writing Evaluation Form (included in this Unit Plan.) Explain to students that during Lesson Nine you will be holding individual conferences about this writing assignment. Make sure they are familiar with the criteria on the Writing Evaluation Form.

Follow-Up: After you have graded the assignments, have a writing conference with each student. (This unit schedules one in Lesson Nine.) After the writing conference, allow students to revise their papers using your suggestions to complete the revision. I suggest grading the revisions on an A-C-E scale (all revisions well-done, some revisions made, few or no revisions made.) This will speed your grading time and still give some credit for the students' efforts.

LESSON SIX

Objectives
1. To review the main ideas and events in Chapters 8-10
2. To preview the study questions and vocabulary for Chapters 11-13
3. To read Chapters 11-13 silently

Activity #1
Ask students to get out their books and some paper (not their study guides.) Tell students to write down ten questions and answers which cover the main events and ideas in Chapter 8-10. Discuss the students' questions and answers orally, making a list on the board of the questions with brief responses. Put a star next to students' questions and answers that are essentially the same as the study guide questions. Be sure that all of the study guide questions are answered.

Activity #2
Give students about fifteen minutes to do the prereading and vocabulary work for Chapters 11-13, then give students the remainder of the period to begin silently reading Chapters 11-13. Remind them that the reading must be completed prior to your next class meeting.

WRITING ASSIGNMENT 1 - *Things Fall Apart*

PROMPT
Many changes happened in Okonkso's village and the surrounding areas. You, as a young member of the village, want to institute yet another change.

Your assignment is to think of a change you would make in the daily life/customs of the village. Present your ideas to the *egwugwu* to persuade them to approve of your idea.

PREWRITING
The first thing you need to do is make a list of the ceremonies and traditions of the villagers. Include things like the number of wives the men have, how the bride-price is agreed upon, how the villagers settle disputes. Then think of something you would like to add or change. Perhaps you are a young girl who wants to choose her own husband, or a young boy who prefers cooking and watching the children to hunting and going to war.

Next, make a list of all of the reasons that your change is beneficial to you personally, and to the clan. Think about how you would implement your change. Tell what you think the results of the change would be.

DRAFTING
Write as if you were at a village meeting, addressing the *egwugwu*. How would you bring up your subject? Use this as your opening paragraph. Then write one paragraph for each of your arguments, using the things that support your statements to fill out the paragraphs. What would you say in closing your speech to convince the *egwugwu* of the merits of your plan? Use that as your closing paragraph.

PROMPT
When you finish the rough draft of your paper, ask another student to read it. After reading your rough draft, he/she should tell you what he/she liked best about your work, which parts were difficult to understand, and ways in which your work could be improved. Reread your paper considering your critic's comments, and make the corrections you think are necessary.

PROOFREADING
Do a final proofreading of your paper, double-checking your grammar, spelling, organization, and the clarity of your ideas.

WRITING EVALUATION FORM - *Things Fall Apart*

Name_____Date_____Class_____

Writing Assignment #1 for *Things Fall Apart*

Circle One For Each Item:

<u>Introduction</u>	excellent	good	fair	poor
<u>Body Paragraphs</u>	excellent	good	fair	poor
<u>Summary</u>	excellent	good	fair	poor
<u>Grammar</u>	excellent	good	fair	poor (errors noted)
<u>Spelling</u>	excellent	good	fair	poor (errors noted)
<u>Punctuation</u>	excellent	good	fair	poor (errors noted)
<u>Legibility</u>	excellent	good	fair	poor (errors noted)

<u>Strengths:</u>

<u>Weaknesses:</u>

<u>Comments/Suggestions:</u>

LESSON SEVEN

Objectives
    1. To review the main ideas and events from Chapters 11-13
    2. To preview the study questions and vocabulary for Chapters 14-19
    3. To read Chapters 14-19

Activity #1
Review the study guide questions and answers for Chapters 11-13

Activity #2
Give students about fifteen minutes to complete the prereading and vocabulary work for Chapters 14-19.

Activity #3
Depending on the needs of your group, have the students read these chapters orally or silently. Remind them that any reading not completed in class must be finished before the next class meeting.

LESSON EIGHT

Objectives
    1. To check to see that students have done the required reading
    2. To introduce Writing Assignment #2

Activity #1
Give students a quiz on Chapters 14-19. Use either the short answer or multiple choice form of the study guide questions as a quiz so that in discussing the answers to the quiz you also answer the study guide questions. Collect the papers for grading.

Activity #2
Distribute Writing Assignment #2. Discuss the directions in detail and give students ample time to complete the assignment.

LESSON NINE

Objectives
    1. To have students revise their first writing assignment papers
    2. To work on other assignments independently

Activities
Call students to your desk or some other private area to discuss their papers from Writing Assignment #1. Use the completed Writing Evaluation Form as a basis for your critique.

Students should use this period (when they are not conferencing with you) to work on their Nonfiction assignment, or to review the study guide questions they have covered so far.

WRITING ASSIGNMENT #2 - *Things Fall Apart*

PROMPT
You are a missionary, trying to build interest in the Christian faith in a village in Africa. Every month you must write a report to your superiors. You must include statistics on the number of converts you have made, which buildings have been constructed and which need to be done, how many students you are teaching, and how many sick patients you have treated. You must also report about any difficulties you are having. Your superiors enjoy seeing drawings and/or photographs. They also like graphs about your progress.

PREWRITING
One way to begin is to jot down your thoughts and ideas about each of the parts of the assignment. You may want to use a word web or an outline to help organize your thoughts. Then re-read the sections of the book that deal with those topics. Add any new information to your list or web. Decide whether or not to include a drawing. If you include one, you will need to look in reference books to see what the Niger area in Africa really looks like, or will you just use your imagination? Decide whether or not to include a graph, and what information to put on it.

DRAFTING
Use your web or outline to decide how to organize your report. The beginning paragraph should be an introduction, stating the purpose of your report. Use a paragraph for each of the topics you discuss. Make sure to include details about your work. Use ideas from the book to make your report sound authentic. Include a paragraph telling how you feel about your work. In another paragraph, present your plans for the next few months. Request any supplies or assistance that you need. End your report with a positive comment about the work.

PROMPT
When you finish the rough draft of your paper, ask a student who sits near you to read it. After reading your rough draft, he/she should tell you what he/she liked best about your work, which parts were difficult to understand, and ways in which your work could be improved. Reread your paper considering your critic's comments, and make the corrections you think are necessary.

PROOFREADING
Do a final proofreading of your paper double-checking your grammar, spelling, organization, and the clarity of your ideas.

LESSON TEN

Objectives
1. To complete the prereading and vocabulary work for Chapters 20-25
2. To silently read Chapters 20-25
3. To review the main ideas and events from Chapters 20-25
4. To make sure the students have the answers to all of the previous study guide questions

Activity #1
Give students about fifteen minutes to preview the study questions and do the related vocabulary work.

Activity #2
Have students read the chapters silently and answer the study guide questions.

Activity #3
Go over the study guide questions for Chapters 20-25.

LESSON ELEVEN

Objectives
      To discuss *Things Fall Apart* at the interpretive and critical levels.

Activity #1
Choose the questions from the Extra Writing Assignments/Discussion Questions which seem most appropriate for your students. A class discussion of these questions is most effective if students have been given the opportunity to formulate answers to the questions prior to the discussion. To this end, you may either have all the students formulate answers to all the questions, divide the class into groups and assign one or more questions to each group, or you could assign one question to each student in your class. The option you choose will make a difference in the amount of class time needed for this activity.

Activity #2
After students have had ample time to formulate answers to the questions, begin your class discussion of the questions and the ideas presented by the questions. Be sure students take notes during the discussion so they have information to study for the unit test.

EXTRA WRITING ASSIGNMENT/DISCUSSION QUESTIONS - *Things Fall Apart*

<u>Interpretive</u>

1. From what point of view is the novel written? How does this affect your understanding of the story?

2. Discuss Okonkwo's views on society, especially manliness.

3. Discuss the main themes in the novel.

4. What does Okonkwo's reaction to the poor yam crop tell about his personality?

5. Discuss the type of family structure portrayed in the novel.

6. What does Okonkwo's treatment of his family tell about his personality?

7. Compare and contrast Nwoye's feelings about the stories his mother tells and those his father tells.

8. The villagers used the words "white skin" when talking about leprosy. How was the coming of the white man like leprosy to the Africans?

9. Discuss the use of emotions in the novel.

10. Did Obierika's observations about Okonkwo's part in the murder of Ikemefuna have any influence on Okonkwo's later life? If so, how?

11. Compare and contrast the Christian religion and that of the villagers.

12. What did Okonkwo mean when he said "living fire begets cold, impotent ash?"

13. Where is the climax of the novel? Justify your answer.

14. Which events in the novel are "turning points" which affect the course of the plot?

15. Discuss the role of superstition in the lives of the villagers.

Extra Writing Assignment/Discussion Questions - *Things Fall Apart*, p. 2

Critical

16. What is foreshadowing? Discuss the use of foreshadowing in the novel.

17. Explain the significance of the title *Things Fall Apart.*

18. What purpose do the folk tales in the story serve?

19. Do any of the characters change in the course of the novel? If so, who, and how?

20. *Things Fall Apart* has been compared to the great Greek tragedies. Do you agree or disagree? Justify your answer.

21. Discuss the use and effectiveness of irony in the novel.

22. Discuss the use of proverbs in the novel. Which ones were particularly effective? Which were ineffective?

23. Discuss the effectiveness of the use of darkness in the novel.

Personal Response

24. Did you enjoy the novel? Why or why not?

25. If you were Chinua Achebe's editor, what changes would you suggest? Why?

26. Would you recommend this book to a friend?

27. How did you feel about Okonkwo as a person?

28. How did you feel about the Christian missionaries?

29. Did you like the ending of the novel? Why or why not?

30. Okonkwo was described as a "strong man." Was he, in your opinion, strong? Justify your answer.

QUOTATIONS - *Things Fall Apart*

Discuss the significance of the following quotations.

1. Among the Ibo the art of conversation is regarded very highly, and proverbs are the palm-oil with which words are eaten.

2. "Our elders say that the sun will shine on those who stand, before it shines on those who kneel under them."

3. Age was respected among his people, but achievement was revered. As the elders said, if a child washed his hands he could eat with kings.

4. It was the fear of himself, lest he should be found to resemble his father.

5. "And when a man is at peace with his gods and his ancestors, his harvest will be good or bad according to the strength of his arm."

6. "*Nna ayi*," he said. "I have brought you this little kola. As our people say, a man who pays respect to the great paves the way for his own greatness."

7. Anyone seeing Chielo in ordinary life would hardly believe she was the same person who prophesied when the spirit of Agbala was upon her.

8. Nwoye knew that it was right to be masculine and to be violent, but somehow he still preferred the stories that his mother used to tell, and which she no doubt still told to her younger children.

9. "Yes, Umuofia has decided to kill him. The Oracle of the Hills and the Caves has pronounced it. They will take him outside Umuofia as is the custom, and kill him there. But I want you to have nothing to do with it. He calls you father."

10. How could she know that Ekwefi's bitterness did not flow outwards to others but inwards into her own soul; that she did not blame others for their good fortune but her own evil *chi* who denied her?

11. The priestess screamed, "Beware, Okonkwo!" she warned. "Beware of exchanging words with Agbala. Does a man speak when a god speaks? Beware!"

12. The land of the living was not far removed from the domain of the ancestors. There was coming and going between them, especially at festivals and also when an old man died, because an old man was very close to the ancestors.

Quotations - *Things Fall Apart*, p. 2

13. And if the clan did not exact punishment for an offense against the great goddess, her wrath was loosed on all the land and not just on the offender. As the elders said, if one finger brought oil it soiled the others.

14. But it was like beginning life anew without the vigor and enthusiasm of youth, like learning to become left-handed in old age.

15. "It's true that a child belongs to its father, but when a father beats his child, it seeks sympathy in its mother's hut. A man belongs to his fatherland when things are good and life is sweet. But when there is sorrow and bitterness he finds refuge in his motherland. Your mother is there to protect you. She is buried there. And that is why we say that mother is supreme."

16. "Those were good days when a man had friends in distant clans. Your generation does not know that. You stay at home, afraid of your next-door neighbor. Even a man's motherland is strange to him nowadays."

17. "The world has no end, and what is good among one people is an abomination with others."

18. "We have been sent by this great God to ask you to leave your wicked ways and false gods and turn to him so that you may be saved when you die," he said.

19. "We do not ask for wealth because he that has health and children will also have wealth. We do not pray to have more money but to have more kinsmen. We are better than animals because we have kinsmen."

20. "You do not know what it is to speak with one voice. And what is the result? An abominable religion has settled among you. A man can now leave his father and his brothers. He can curse the gods of his fathers and his ancestors, like a hunter's dog that suddenly turns on his master. I fear for you; I fear for the clan."

21. The clan was like a lizard; if it lost its tail it soon grew another.

22. "How do you think we can fight when our own brothers have turned against us? The white man is very clever. He came quietly and peaceably with his religion. We were amused at his foolishness and allowed him to stay. Now he has won our brothers, and our clan can no longer act like one. He has put a knife on the things that held us together and we have fallen apart."

Quotations - *Things Fall Apart,* p. 3

23. "Worthy men are no more," Okonkwo sighed as he remembered those days. "Isike will never forget how we slaughtered them in that war. We killed twelve of their men and they killed only two of ours. Before the end of the fourth market week they were suing for peace. Those were the days when men were men."

24. "All our gods are weeping, Idemili is weeping, Ogwuguw is weeping, Agbala is weeping, and all the others. Our dead fathers are weeping because of the shameful sacrilege they are suffering and the abomination we have all seen with our eyes."

25. "We must root out this evil. And if our brothers take the side of evil we must root them out, too. And we must do it *now*. We must bale this water now that it is only ankle-deep...."

26. "That man was one of the greatest men in Umuofia. You drove him to kill himself; and now he will be buried like a dog."

27. He had already chosen the title of the book, after much thought: *The Pacification of the Primitive Tribes of the Lower Niger.*

LESSON TWELVE

Objectives
1. To introduce Writing Assignment #3
2. To give students time to work on the writing assignment

Activity #1

Distribute copies of Writing Assignment #3. Discuss the directions in detail and give students ample time to complete the assignment.

LESSON THIRTEEN

Objectives
1. To give students the opportunity to do research for their Nonfiction Assignment
2. To assist students in the proper use of the school library

Activity

Take your class to the library for the entire class period. Tell them they can have the time to work on their Nonfiction Assignment. Students who have completed the assignment can use the time to read for pleasure.

LESSON FOURTEEN

Objectives
1. To widen the breadth of students' knowledge about the topics discussed or touched upon in *Things Fall Apart*
2. To check students' non-fiction assignments

Activity

Ask each student to give a brief oral report about the nonfiction work he/she read for the nonfiction assignment. Your criteria for evaluating this report will vary depending on the level of your students. You may wish for students to give a complete report without using notes of any kind, or you may want students to read directly from a written report, or you may want to do something in between these two extremes. Just make students aware of your criteria in ample time for them to prepare their reports.

Start with one student's report. After that, ask if anyone else in the class has read on a topic related to the first student's report. If no one has, choose another student at random. After each report, be sure to ask if anyone has a report related to the one just completed. That will help keep a continuity during the discussion of the reports.

WRITING ASSIGNMENT #3 - *Things Fall Apart*

PROMPT
Many changes occurred throughout the novel. Okonkwo and some others did not like the changes. Other villagers did seem to like the new ways of the white men. Your assignment is to write about a change you had in your life. Tell how it affected you, and whether or not you think the change was for the better.

PREWRITING
Make a time line of the important events in your life that involved changes. Death, birth, divorce, and moving are all major changes that occur in people's lives. Other changes include getting a new hair style, getting your first job or a new job, getting a driver's license, transferring to a new school. You can probably think of many others. Choose the change you want to write about. You may want to interview a relative or friend who knew you before and after the change occurred, to get their perspective on how the change affected you. Spend some time remembering what was going on in your life at the time of the change. Write down your feelings and impressions.

DRAFTING
Organize your ideas into a rough outline. In the first paragraph, give some background about yourself, and your life before the change occurred. In the next paragraph, describe the change. Use another paragraph to explain how the change affected you. In your concluding paragraph, tell whether you think the change was good or not, and state your reasons.

PROMPT
After you have finished a rough draft of your paper, revise it until you are happy with your work. Then ask another student to tell you what he/she likes best about your work, and what things she/he thinks can be improved. Take another look at your work, keeping in mind your critic's suggestions, and make the revisions you feel are necessary.

PROOFREADING
Do a final proofreading of your paper, double-checking your grammar, spelling, organization, and the clarity of your ideas.

LESSON FIFTEEN

Objectives
To review all of the vocabulary work done in this unit

VOCABULARY REVIEW ACTIVITIES

1. Divide your class into two teams and have an old-fashioned spelling or definition bee.

2. Give each of your students (or students in groups of two, three or four) a *Things Fall Apart* Vocabulary Word Search Puzzle. The person (group) to find all of the vocabulary words in the puzzle first wins.

3. Give students a *Things Fall Apart* Vocabulary Word Search Puzzle without the word list. The person or group to find the most vocabulary words in the puzzle wins.

4. Use a *Things Fall Apart* Vocabulary Crossword Puzzle. Put the puzzle onto a transparency on the overhead projector (so everyone can see it), and do the puzzle together as a class.

5. Give students a *Things Fall Apart* Vocabulary Matching Worksheet to do.

6. Divide your class into two teams. Use the *Things Fall Apart* vocabulary words with their letters jumbled as a word list. Student 1 from Team A faces off against Student 1 from Team B. You write the first jumbled word on the board. The first student (1A or 1B) to unscramble the word wins the chance for his/her team to score points. If 1A wins the jumble, go to student 2A and give him/her a definition. He/she must give you the correct spelling of the vocabulary word which fits that definition. If he/she does, Team A scores a point, and you give student 3A a definition for which you expect a correctly spelled matching vocabulary word. Continue giving Team A definitions until some team member makes an incorrect response. An incorrect response sends the game back to the jumbled-word face off, this time with students 2A and 2B. Instead of repeating giving definitions to the first few students of each team, continue with the student after the one who gave the last incorrect response on the team. For example, if team B wins the jumbled-word face-off, and student 5B gave the last incorrect answer for team B, you would start this round of definition questions with student 6B, and so on. The team with the most points wins!

7. Have students write a story in which they correctly use as many vocabulary words as possible. Have students read their compositions orally. Post the most original compositions on your bulletin board.

LESSON SIXTEEN

Objective
To review the main ideas presented in *Things Fall Apart*

Activity #1
Choose one of the review games/activities included in the packet and spend your class period as outlined there.

Activity #2
Remind students of the date for the Unit Test. Stress the review of the Study Guides and their class notes as a last minute, brush-up review for homework.

REVIEW GAMES/ACTIVITIES

1. Ask the class to make up a unit test for *Things Fall Apart*. The test should have 4 sections: multiple choice, true/false, short answer and essay. Students may use ½ period to make the test, including a separate answer sheet, and then swap papers and use the other ½ class period to take a test a classmate has devised (open book).

2. Take ½ period for students to make up true and false questions (including the answers). Collect the papers and divide the class into two teams. Draw a big tic-tac-toe board on the chalk board. Make one team X and one team O. Ask questions to each side, giving each student one turn. If the question is answered correctly, that student's team's letter (X or O) is placed in the box. If the answer is incorrect, no mark is placed in the box. The object is to get three marks in a row like tic-tac-toe. You may want to keep track of the number of games won for each team.

3. Take ½ period for students to make up questions (true/false and short answer). Collect the questions. Divide the class into two teams. You'll alternate asking questions to individual members of teams A & B (like in a spelling bee). The question keeps going from A to B until it is correctly answered, then a new question is asked. A correct answer does not allow the team to get another question. Correct answers are + 2 points; incorrect answers are - 1 point.

4. Allow students time to quiz each other (in pairs) from their study guides and class notes.

5. Give students a *Things Fall Apart* crossword puzzle to complete.

Review Games/Activities - *Things Fall Apart*, p. 2

6. Divide your class into two teams. Use the *Things Fall Apart* crossword words with their letters jumbled as a word list. Student 1 from Team A faces off against Student 1 from Team B. You write the first jumbled word on the board. The first student (1A or 1B) to unscramble the word wins the chance for his/her team to score points. If 1A wins the jumble, go to student 2A and give him/her a clue. He/she must give you the correct word which matches that clue. If he/she does, Team A scores a point, and you give student 3A a clue for which you expect another correct response. Continue giving Team A clues until some team member makes an incorrect response. An incorrect response sends the game back to the jumbled-word face-off, this time with students 2A and 2B. Instead of repeating giving clues to the first few students of each team, continue with the student after the one who gave the last incorrect response on the team.

7. Take on the persona of "The Answer Person." Allow students to ask any question about the book. Answer the questions, or tell students where to look in the book to find the answer.

8. Students may enjoy playing charades with events from the story. Select a student to start. Give him/her a card with a scene or event from the story. Allow the players to use their books to find the scene being described. The first person to guess each charade performs the next one.

9. Play a categories-type quiz game. (A master is included in this Unit Plan.) Make an overhead transparency of the categories form. Divide the class into teams of three or four players each Have each team choose a recorder and a banker. Choose a team to go first. That team will choose a category and point amount. Ask the question to the entire class. (Use the Study Guide Quiz and Vocabulary questions). Give the teams one minute to discuss the answer and write it down. Walk around the room and check the answers. Each team that answers correctly receives the points.(Incorrect answers are not penalized; they just don't receive any points). Cross out that square on the playing board. Play continues until all squares have been used. The winning team is the one with the most points. You can assign bonus points to any square or squares you choose.

10. Have students complete the last column (What I Learned) of the KWL sheet you distributed in Lesson One. Discuss their answers with the class.

NOTE: If students do not need the extra review, omit this lesson and go on to the test.

QUIZ GAME - *Things Fall Apart*

100	100	100	100	100	100
200	200	200	200	200	200
300	300	300	300	300	300
400	400	400	400	400	400
500	500	500	500	500	500

LESSON SEVENTEEN

Objectives
   To test the students' understanding of the main ideas and themes in *Things Fall Apart*

Activity #1
Distribute the *Things Fall Apart* Unit Tests. Go over the instructions in detail and allow the students the entire class period to complete the exam.

Activity #2
Collect all test papers and assigned books prior to the end of the class period.

NOTES ABOUT THE UNIT TESTS IN THIS UNIT:

There are 5 different unit tests which follow.

There are two short answer tests which are based primarily on facts from the novel. The answer key for short answer unit test 1 follows the student test. The answer key for short answer test 2 follows the student short answer unit test 2.

There is one advanced short answer unit test. It is based on the extra discussion questions. Use the matching key for short answer unit test 2 to check the matching section of the advanced short answer unit test. There is no key for the short answer questions. The answers will be based on the discussions you have had during class.

There are two multiple choice unit tests. Following the two unit tests, you will find an answer sheet on which students should mark their answers. The same answer sheet should be used for both tests; however, students' answers will be different for each test. Following the students' answer sheet for the multiple choice tests you will find your answer keys.

The short answer tests have a vocabulary section. You should choose 10 of the vocabulary words from this unit, read them orally and have the students write them down. Then, either have students write a definition, or use the words in sentences.

UNIT TESTS

SHORT ANSWER UNIT TEST 1 - *Things Fall Apart*

1. Matching/Identification

    ____ 1. Unoka   A. Okonkwo's lazy son

    ____ 2. Umuofia   B. major god of the villagers

    ____ 3. Ezinma   C. village where Okonkwo lived

    ____ 4. Nwoye   D. village where Okonkwo went into exile

    ____ 5. Obierika   E. Okonkwo's favorite child

    ____ 6. Chukwu   F. young boy who was murdered by the clan

    ____ 7. Chielo   G. Okonkwo's friend

    ____ 8. Mbanta   H. first missionary in Umuofia

    ____ 9. Mr. Brown   I. Okonkwo's unsuccessful father

    ____ 10. Ikemefuna   J. priestess for the oracle

II. Short Answer

1. How did the people view yams?

2. Describe Okonkwo's physical appearance and personality.

Short Answer Unit Test 1 *Things Fall Apart*, p. 2

3. What did Okonkwo do whenever he thought of his father's weakness and failure?

4. Describe what happened to Ikemefuna.

5. Describe the search for Ezinma's *iyi-uwa*, and explain its significance.

6. Describe the events that happened at Ezeudu's funeral.

Short Answer Unit Test 1 *Things Fall Apart*, p. 3

7. Where did the missionaries in Mbanta build their church, why were they given that particular piece of land, and what happened to them?

8. Describe the changes that had come to Umuofia in the seven years that Okonkwo was in exile.

9. How did Okonkwo feel when he returned from the white man's prison?

10. What happened to Okonkwo at the end of the story?

Short Answer Unit Test 1 *Things Fall Apart*, p. 4

III. Essay

Explain the significance of the title *Things Fall Apart*.

Short Answer Unit Test 1 *Things Fall Apart*, p. 5

IV. Vocabulary

Listen to the vocabulary word and spell it. After you have spelled all the words, go back and write down the definitions.

WORD	DEFINITION
1. _____	_____
2. _____	_____
3. _____	_____
4. _____	_____
5. _____	_____
6. _____	_____
7. _____	_____
8. _____	_____
9. _____	_____
10. _____	_____
11. _____	_____
12. _____	_____
13. _____	_____
14. _____	_____
15. _____	_____
16. _____	_____
17. _____	_____
18. _____	_____
19. _____	_____
20. _____	_____

ANSWER KEY SHORT ANSWER UNIT TEST 1 - *Things Fall Apart*

1. Matching/Identification

   I 1. Unoka   A. Okonkwo's lazy son
   C 2. Umuofia   B. major god of the villagers
   E 3. Ezinma   C. village where Okonkwo lived
   A 4. Nwoye   D. village where Okonkwo went into exile
   G 5. Obierika   E. Okonkwo's favorite child
   B 6. Chukwu   F. young boy who was murdered by the clan
   J 7. Chielo   G. Okonkwo's friend
   D 8. Mbanta   H. first missionary in Umuofia
   H 9. Mr. Brown   I. Okonkwo's unsuccessful father
   F 10. Ikemefuna   J. priestess for the oracle

II. Short Answer

1. How did the people view yams?
   Yams stood for manliness, and one who could feed his family on yams all year was a great man.

2. Describe Okonkwo's physical appearance and personality.
   He was tall and huge. His bushy eyebrows and wide nose made him look severe. He walked as though he were ready to pounce. He was impatient, and quick to anger. Okonkwo was hard-working, and had a large crop of yams.

3. What did Okonwo do whenever he thought of his father's weakness and failure?
   He thought of his own strength and success.

4. Describe what happened to Ikemefuna.
   The oracle decided that the villagers should kill him. The men told him he was going home, and they all left the village. One of the men struck Ikemefuna from behind. When he called out to Okonkwo that he had been killed, Okonkwo panicked and killed him with his machete.

5. Describe the search for Ezinma's *iyi-uwa*, and explain its significance.
   This was a special kind of stone that formed the link between an *ogbanje* and the spirit world. If it were discovered, then the child would not die. Ezinma didn't really know what they were talking about, but she dutifully led Okagbue and the others through the bush, then back to the road. She pointed to a spot under an orange tree and said her *iyi-uwa* was there. Okagbue and Okonkwo dug until they found a stone wrapped in a cloth, which Okagbue said was the *iyi-uwa*. Then the people knew Ezinma's troubles were over.

Answer Key Short Answer Test 1 *Things Fall Apart*, p. 2

6. Describe the events that happened at Ezeudu's funeral.
   He was the clan elder, so there was a great ceremony. There was a lot of shouting, drum beating, and firing of guns. Okonko accidentally shot a boy and killed him.

7. Where did the missionaries in Mbanta build their church, why were they given that particular piece of land, and what happened to them?
   The villagers gave the missionaries land in the Evil Forest, because they didn't really want them, and they thought the missionaries would decline the offer. When the missionaries were alive and well when the villagers expected them to be dead, they won more converts.

8. Describe the changes that had come to Umuofia in the seven years that Okonkwo was in exile.
   The Christian church had many converts. The white men had brought a government and built a court. The new prison was full of men who had broken the white men's laws.

9. How did Okonkwo feel when he returned from the white man's prison?
   He was full of hate and bitterness, and wanted revenge.

10. What happened to Okonkwo at the end of the story?
    He hanged himself.

SHORT ANSWER UNIT TEST 2 - *Things Fall Apart*

1. Matching/Identify

　　　 1. Obierika　　　　　　　A. Okonkwo's unsuccessful father
　　　 2. Ikemefuna　　　　　　 B. first missionary in Umuofia
　　　 3. Nwoye　　　　　　　　C. Okonkwo's favorite child
　　　 4. Ezinma　　　　　　　　D. young boy who was murdered by the clan
　　　 5. Chielo　　　　　　　　 E. village where Okonkwo went into exile
　　　 6. Mr. Brown　　　　　　 F. Okonkwo's friend
　　　 7. Chukwu　　　　　　　 G. Okonkwo's lazy son
　　　 8. Unoka　　　　　　　　 H. priestess for the oracle
　　　 9. Umuofia　　　　　　　 I. major god of the villagers
　　　10. Mbanta　　　　　　　　J. village where Okonkwo lived

II. Short Answer

1. Describe what happened to Ikemefuna.

2. Describe the changes that had come to Umuofia in the seven years that Okonkwo was in exile.

Short Answer Unit Test 2 *Things Fall Apart*, p. 2

3. Describe Okonkwo's physical appearance and personality.

4. Describe the search for Ezinma's *iyi-uwa*, and explain its significance.

5. What happened to Okonkwo at the end of the story?

6. Where did the missionaries in Mbanta build their church, why were they given that particular piece of land, and what happened to them?

Short Answer Unit Test 2 *Things Fall Apart*, p. 3

7. Describe the events that happened at Ezeudu's funeral.

8. What did Okonkwo do whenever he thought of his father's weakness and failure?

9. How did Okonkwo feel when he returned from the white man's prison?

10. How did the people view yams?

Short Answer Unit Test 2 *Things Fall Apart*, p. 4

III. Essay   Do any of the characters change in the course of the novel? If so, who, and how?

Short Answer Unit Test 2 *Things Fall Apart*, p. 5
IV. Vocabulary
Listen to the vocabulary word and spell it. After you have spelled all the words, go back and write down the definitions.

WORD	DEFINITION
1.	
2.	
3.	
4.	
5.	
6.	
7.	
8.	
9.	
10.	
11.	
12.	
13.	
14.	
15.	
16.	
17.	
18.	
19.	
20.	

ANSWER KEY SHORT ANSWER UNIT TEST 2 - *Things Fall Apart*

Use this answer key for Short Answer Unit Test 2 and the Advanced Short Answer Unit Test.

1. Matching/Identify

F	1. Obierika	A.	Okonkwo's unsuccessful fahter
D	2. Ikemefuna	B.	first missionary in Umuofia
G	3. Nwoye	C.	Okonkwo's favorite child
C	4. Ezinma	D.	young boy who was murdered by the clan
H	5. Chielo	E.	village where Okonkwo went into exile
B	6. Mr. Brown	F.	Okonkwo's friend
I	7. Chukwu	G.	Okonkwo's lazy son
A	8. Unoka	H.	priestess for the oracle
J	9. Umuofia	I.	major god of the villagers
E	10. Mbanta	J.	village where Okonkwo lived

II. Short Answer

1. Describe what happened to Ikemefuna.
   The oracle decided that the villagers should kill him. The men told him he was going home, and they all left the village. One of the men struck Ikemefuna from behind. When he called out to Okonkwo that he had been killed, Okonkwo panicked and killed him with his machete.

2. Describe the changes that had come to Umuofia in the seven years that Okonkwo was in exile.
   The Christian church had many converts. The white men had brought a government and built a court. The new prison was full of men who had broken the white men's laws.

3. Describe Okonkwo's physical appearance and personality.
   He was tall and huge. His bushy eyebrows and wide nose made him look severe. He walked as though he were ready to pounce. He was impatient, and quick to anger. Okonkwo was hard-working, and had a large crop of yams.

4. Describe the search for Ezinma's *iyi-uwa*, and explain its significance.
   This was a special kind of stone that formed the link between an *ogbanje* and the spirit world. If it were discovered, then the child would not die. Ezinma didn't really know what they were talking about, but she dutifully led Okagbue and the others through the bush, then back to the road. She pointed to a spot under an orange tree and said her *iyi-uwa* was there. Okagbue and Okonkwo dug until they found a stone wrapped in a cloth, which Okagbue said was the *iyi-uwa*. Then the people knew Ezinma's troubles were over.

5. What happened to Okonkwo at the end of the story?
   He hanged himself.

Answer Key Short Answer Unit Test 2 *Things Fall Apart*, p. 2

6. Where did the missionaries in Mbanta build their church, why were they given that particular piece of land, and what happened to them?
   The villagers gave the missionaries land in the Evil Forest, because they didn't really want them, and they thought the missionaries would decline the offer. When the missionaries were alive and well when the villagers expected them to be dead, they won more converts.

7. Describe the events that happened at Ezeudu's funeral.
   He was the clan elder, so there was a great ceremony. There was a lot of shouting, drum beating, and firing of guns. Okonkwo accidentally shot a boy and killed him.

8. What did Okonkwo do whenever he thought of his father's weakness and failure?
   He thought of his own strength and success.

9. How did Okonkwo feel when he returned from the white man's prison?
   He was full of hate and bitterness, and wanted revenge.

10. How did the people view yams?
    Yams stood for manliness, and one who could feed his family on yams all year was a great man.

ADVANCED SHORT ANSWER UNIT TEST - *Things Fall Apart*

1. Matching/Identify

   ____ 1. Obierika   A. Okonkwo's unsuccessful father
   ____ 2. Ikemefuna   B. first missionary in Umuofia
   ____ 3. Nwoye   C. Okonkwo's favorite child
   ____ 4. Ezinma   D. young boy who was murdered by the clan
   ____ 5. Chielo   E. village where Okonkwo went into exile
   ____ 6. Mr. Brown   F. Okonkwo's friend
   ____ 7. Chukwu   G. Okonkwo's lazy son
   ____ 8. Unoka   H. priestess for the oracle
   ____ 9. Umuofia   I. major god of the villagers
   ____ 10. Mbanta   J. village where Okonkwo lived

II. Short Answer

1. What is foreshadowing? Describe the use of foreshadowing in the novel.

Advanced Answer Unit Test *Things Fall Apart*, p. 2

2. Explain the significance of the title *Things Fall Apart*.

3. Discuss the use and effectivenss of irony in the novel.

Advanced Answer Unit Test *Things Fall Apart,* p. 3

4. Discuss Okonkwo's views on life, especially manliness.

5. The villagers used the words "white skin" when talking about leprosy. How was the coming of the white man like leprosy to the Africans?

Advanced Answer Unit Test *Things Fall Apart*, p. 4

III. Quotations
Identify the speaker and discuss the significance of each of the following quotations.

1. "Yes, Umuofia has decided to kill him. The Oracle of the Hills and the Caves has pronounced it. They will take him outside Umuofia as is the custom, and kill him there. But I want you to have nothing to do with it. He calls you father."

2. "It's true that a child belongs to its father, but when a father beats his child, it seeks sympathy in its mother's hut. A man belongs to his fatherland when things are good and life is sweet. But when there is sorrow and bitterness he finds refuge in his motherland. Your mother is there to protect you. She is buried there. And that is why we say that mother is supreme."

3. "Those were good days when a man had friends in distant clans. Your generation does not know that. You stay at home, afraid of your next-door neighbor. Even a man's motherland is strange to him nowadays."

Advanced Answer Unit Test *Things Fall Apart,* p. 5

4. "You do not know what it is to speak with one voice. And what is the result? An abominable religion has settled among you. A man can now leave his father and his brothers. He can curse the gods of his fathers and ancestors, like a hunter's dog that suddenly turns on his master. I fear for you; I fear for the clan."

5. He had already chosen the title of the book, after much thought: *The Pacification of the Primitive Tribes of the Lower Niger.*

Advanced Answer Unit Test *Things Fall Apart,* p. 6

IV. Vocabulary

Listen to the vocabulary words and write them down. After you have written down all of the words, write a paragraph in which you use all the words. The paragraph must in some way relate to *Things Fall Apart.*

MULTIPLE CHOICE UNIT TEST 1 *Things Fall Apart*

Matching/Identification

____ 1.	Unoka	A.	Okonkwo's lazy son
____ 2.	Umuofia	B.	major god of the villagers
____ 3.	Ezinma	C.	village where Okonkwo lived
____ 4.	Nwoye	D.	village where Okonkwo went into exile
____ 5.	Obierika	E.	Okonkwo's favorite child
____ 6.	Chukwu	F.	young boy who was murdered by the clan
____ 7.	Chielo	G.	Okonkwo's friend
____ 8.	Mbanta	H.	first missionary in Umuofia
____ 9.	Mr. Brown	I.	Okonkwo's unsuccessful father
____ 10.	Ikemefuna	J.	priestess for the oracle

II. Multiple Choice

1. What food stood for manliness, and was a sign of prosperity?
    A. It was potatoes.
    B. It was yams.
    C. It was coconuts.
    D. It was plantains.

2. Who struck the last blow to *Ikemefuna*, and why?
    A. Okonkwo did, because he was afraid of being thought weak.
    B. Nwoye did, to please his father.
    C. Ogbuefi Ezeudu did, because he was the oldest man in the village.
    D. Obierika did, because he didn't like Ikemefuna.

3. What did Okonkwo do whenever he thought of his father's weakness and failure?
    A. He beat a few of his children.
        B. He got drunk for a few days.
    C. He thought of his own strength and success.
    D. He prayed to his ancestral gods for strength.

4. What was Ezinma's *iyi-uwa*, or link with the *ogbanje*?
    A. It was a birth-mark, like a mole, that had to be removed.
    B. It was a special kind of stone that was buried in the ground.
    C. It was a yam seed that was square in shape.
    D. It was a cowry shell that was a different color than the rest.

Multiple Choice Unit Test 1 *Things Fall Apart*, p. 2

5. Who wanted to take Ezinma to see Agbala?
   A. Obierika did.
   B. The other wives did.
   C. Nwoye did.
   D. Chielo did. B.

6. Which did **not** happen during Ezudu's funeral?
   A. There was a lot of shouting.
   B. There was a lot of drum beating.
   C. The men and boys had wrestling matches.
   D. The men fired their guns.

7. True or False: The author describes a man's life as a continual struggle to get away from his ancestors.
   A. True
   B. False

8. True or False: The villagers gave the missionaries a piece of the best land in the village because it was their custom to be polite to newcomers.
   A. True
   B. False

9. Which of the following was **not** one of the changes that had come to Umuofia in the seven years that Okonkwo was in exile?
   A. The Christian church had many converts.
   B. The white men had brought a government and built a court.
   C. The new prison was full of men who had broken the white men's law.
   D. The villagers had to pay taxes to the white men.

10. What happened to Okonkwo?
    A. He hanged himself.
    B. He was taken prisoner.
    C. He escaped into the forest.
    D. He finally accepted the white man's rule.

Multiple Choice Unit Test 1 *Things Fall Apart*, p. 3

III Quotations   Identify the speaker:
A. Okonkwo   C. Missionary   E. Chielo
B. Obierika   D. Ezeudu   F. Uchendu

1. *"Nna ayi"* he said, "I have brought you this little kola. As our people say, a man who pays respect to the great, paves the way for his own greatness."

2. "Beware, Okonkwo! Beware of exchanging words with Agbala. Does a man speak when a god speaks? Beware!"

3. "It's true that a child belongs to its father, but when a father beats his child, it seeks sympathy in its mother's hut. A man belongs to his fatherland when things are good and life is sweet. But when there is sorrow and bitterness he finds refuge in his motherland. Your mother is there to protect you. She is buried there. And that is why we say that mother is supreme."

4. "Those were good days when a man had friends in distant clans. Your generation does not know that. You stay at home, afraid of your next-door neighbor. Even a man's motherland is strange to him nowadays."

5. "We have been sent by this great God to ask you to leave your wicked ways and false gods and turn to him so that you may be saved when you die," he said.

6. "We do not ask for wealth because he that has health and children will also have wealth. We do not pray to have more money but to have more kinsmen. We are better than animals because we have kinsmen."

7. "There is no story that is not true. The world has no end, and what is good among one people is an abomination with others."

8. "How do you think we can fight when our own brothers have turned against us? The white man is very clever. He came quietly and peaceably with his religion. We were amused at his foolishness and allowed him to stay. Now he has won our brothers, and our clan can no longer act like one. He has put a knife on the things that held us together and we have fallen apart."

9. "Worthy men are no more. Isike will never forget how we slaughtered them in that war. We killed twelve of their men and they killed only two of ours. Before the end of the fourth market week they were suing for peace. Those were the days when men were men."

10. "That man was one of the greatest men in Umuofia. You drove him to kill himself; and now he will be buried like a dog."

Multiple Choice Unit Test 1 *Things Fall Apart*, p. 4

1. improvident
2. incipient
3. harbingers
4. copiously
5. bouts
6. valor
7. malevolence
8. esoteric
9. impenetrably
10. notorious
11. consolations
12. essences
13. discern
14. diffused
15. callow
16. vile
17. ostracize
18. resilient
19. tumult
20. abominations

A. courage in battle
B. words of comfort
C. loathsome, disgusting
D. detestable things
E. not providing for the future
F. commotion, riot
G. beginning to exist or appear
H. evil or harmful influence
I. spiritual or incorporeal entities
J. exclude from public favor
K. known widely and unfavorably
L. elastic, able to spring back
M. forerunners
N. youthful, immature
O. contests, matches
P. spread in all directions
Q. known only to the chosen few
R. abundantly
S. distinguish, perceive
T. not able to be entered or pierced

MULTIPLE CHOICE UNIT TEST 2 *Things Fall Apart*

I. Matching/Identify
- ____ 1. Obierika
- ____ 2. Ikemefuna
- ____ 3. Nwoye
- ____ 4. Ezinma
- ____ 5. Chielo
- ____ 6. Mr. Brown
- ____ 7. Chukwu
- ____ 8. Unoka
- ____ 9. Umuofia
- ____ 10. Mbanta

A. Okonkwo's unsuccessful father
B. first missionary in Umuofia
C. Okonkwo's favorite child
D. young boy who was murdered by the clan
E. village where Okonkwo went into exile
F. Okonkwo's friend
G. Okonkwo's lazy son
H. priestess for the oracle
I. major god of the villagers
J. village where Okonkwo lived

II. Multiple Choice

1. What food stood for manliness, and was a sign of prosperity?
    A. It was yams.
    B. It was potatoes.
    C. It was coconuts.
    D. It was plantains.

2. Who struck the last blow to Ikemefuna, and why?
    A. Nwoye did, to please his father.
    B. Okonkwo did, because he was afraid of being thought weak.
    C. Ogbuefi Ezeudu did, because he was the oldest man in the village.
    D. Obierika did, because he didn't like Ikemefuna.

3. What did Okonkwo do whenever he thought of his father's weakness and failure?
    A. He beat a few of his children.
    B. He got drunk for a few days.
    C. He thought of his own strength and success.
    D. He prayed to his ancestral gods for strength.

3. What was Ezinma's *iyi-uwa*, or link with the *ogbanje*?
    A. It was a birth-mark, like a mole, that had to be removed.
    B. It was a special kind of stone that was buried in the ground.
    C. It was a yam seed that was square in shape.
    D. It was a cowry shell that was a different color than the rest.

Multiple Choice Unit Test 2 *Things Fall Apart*, p. 2

4. Who wanted to take Ezinma to see Agbala?
   A. Obierika did.
   B. The other wives did.
   C. Nwoye did.
   D. Chielo did.

5. Which did **not** happen during Ezeudu's funeral?
   A There was a lot of shouting.
   B. There was a lot of drum beating.
   C. The men and boys had wrestling matches.
   D. The men fired their guns.

6. True or False: The author describes a man's life as a continual struggle to get away from his ancestors.
   A. True
   B. False

7. True or False: The villagers gave the missionaries a piece of the best land in the village because it was their custom to be polite to newcomers.
   A. True
   B. False

8. Which of the following was **not** one of the changes that had come to Umuofia in the seven years that Okonkwo was in exile?
   A. The new prison was full of men who had broken the white men's laws.
   B. The white men had brought a government and built a court.
   C. The Christian church had many converts.
   D. The villages had to pay taxes to the white men.

9. What happened to Okonkwo?
   A. He finally accepted the white man's rule.
   B. He was taken prisoner.
   C. He escaped into the forest.
   D. He hanged himself.

Multiple Choice Unit Test 2 *Things Fall Apart*, p. 3

III. Quotations   Identify the speaker:

A. Okonkwo   C. Missionary   E. Chielo
B. Obierika   D. Ezeudu   F. Uchendu

1. "It's true that a child belongs to its father, but when a father beats his child, it seeks sympathy in its mother's hut. A man belongs to his fatherland when things are good and life is sweet. But when there is sorrow and bitterness he finds refuge in his motherland. Your mother is there to protect you. She is buried there. And that is why we say that mother is supreme."

2. "We do not ask for wealth because he that has health and children will also have wealth. We do not pray to have more money but to have more kinsmen. We are better than animals because we have kinsmen."

3. "That man was one of the greatest men in Umuofia. You drove him to kill himself; and now he will be buried like a dog."

4. "There is no story that is not true. The world has no end, and what is good among one people is an abomination with others."

5. *"Nna ayi"* he said, "I have brought you this little kola. As our people say, a man who pays respect to the great, paves the way for his own greatness."

6. "Those were good days when a man had friends in distant clans. Your generation does not know that. You stay at home, afraid of your next-door neighbor. Even a man's motherland is strange to him nowadays."

7. "Beware, Okonkwo! Beware of exchanging words with Agbala. Does a man speak when a god speaks? Beware!"

8. "Worthy men are no more. Isike will never forget how we slaughtered them in that war. We killed twelve of their men and they killed only two of ours. Before the end of the fourth market week they were suing for peace. Those were the days when men were men."

9. "We have been sent by this great God to ask you to leave your wicked ways and false gods and turn to him so that you may be saved when you die," he said.

10. "How do you think we can fight when our own brothers have turned against us? The white man is very clever. He came quietly and peaceably with his religion. We were amused at his foolishness and allowed him to stay. Now he has won our brothers, and our clan can no longer act like one. He has put a knife on the things that held us together and we have fallen apart."

Multiple Choice Unit Test 1 *Things Fall Apart*, p. 4

IV. Vocabulary Matching

1. agitated
2. begot
3. approbation
4. capricious
5. communal
6. compromise
7. delectable
8. flourish
9. harbingers
10. frenzy
11. imminent
12. imperious
13. incipient
14. listless
15. miscreant
16. mutilate
17. perturbed
18. rebuked
19. specious
20. prestige

A. impression produced by achievement or reputation
B. greatly disturbed
C. lacking in spirit or energy
D. impending; near at hand
E. grow well; prosper
F. of a group of people
G. approval
H. seemingly reliable but incorrect
I. disfigure or deprive of a limb
J. state of violent mental agitation or wild excitement
K. adjustments
L. produced; fathered
M. criticized or reproved sharply
N. forerunners
O. wretch; villain
P. delightful; delicious
Q. beginning to exist or appear
R. impulsive and unpredictable
S. arrogantly domineering
T. stirred up; disturbed

ANSWER SHEET MULTIPLE CHOICE UNIT TEST - *Things Fall Apart*

I. Matching	III. Quotations	IV. Vocabulary
1. _____	1. _____	1. _____
2. _____	2. _____	2. _____
3. _____	3. _____	3. _____
4. _____	4. _____	4. _____
5. _____	5. _____	5. _____
6. _____	6. _____	6. _____
7. _____	7. _____	7. _____
8. _____	8. _____	8. _____
9. _____	9. _____	9. _____
10. _____	10. _____	10. _____

II. Multiple Choice

1. (A) (B) (C) (D)
2. (A) (B) (C) (D)
3. (A) (B) (C) (D)
4. (A) (B) (C) (D)
5. (A) (B) (C) (D)
6. (A) (B) (C) (D)
7. (A) (B) (C) (D)
8. (A) (B) (C) (D)
9. (A) (B) (C) (D)
10. (A) (B) (C) (D)

11. _____
12. _____
13. _____
14. _____
15. _____
16. _____
17. _____
18. _____
19. _____
20. _____

ANSWER SHEET KEY MULTIPLE CHOICE UNIT TEST 1 - *Things Fall Apart*

I. Matching	III. Quotations	IV. Vocabulary
1. I	1. A	1. E
2. C	2. E	2. G
3. E	3. F	3. M
4. A	4. F	4. R
5. G	5. C	5. O
6. B	6. F	6. A
7. J	7. F	7. H
8. D	8. A	8. Q
9. H	9. A	9. T
10. F	10. B	10. K

II. Multiple Choice

1. B
2. A
3. C
4. B
5. D
6. C
7. B
8. B
9. D
10. A

11. B
12. I
13. S
14. P
15. N
16. C
17. J
18. L
19. F
20. D

ANSWER SHEET KEY MULTIPLE CHOICE UNIT TEST 2 - *Things Fall Apart*

I. Matching	II. Quotations	IV. Vocabulary
1. F	1. F	1. T
2. D	2. F	2. L
3. G	3. B	3. G
4. C	4. F	4. R
5. H	5. A	5. F
6. B	6. F	6. K
7. I	7. E	7. P
8. A	8. A	8. E
9. J	9. C	9. N
10. E	10. A	10. J

II. Multiple Choice
1. A
2. B
3. C
4. B
5. D
6. C
7. B
8. B
9. A
10. D

11. D
12. S
13. Q
14. C
15. O
16. I
17. B
18. M
19. H
20. A

UNIT RESOURCE MATERIALS

BULLETIN BOARD IDEAS *Things Fall Apart*

1. Save one corner of the board for the best of students' *Things Fall Apart* writing assignments. You may want to use background maps of Africa, especially Nigeria, to represent the setting of the novel.

2. Take one of the word search puzzles from the extra activities packet and with a marker copy it over in a large size on the bulletin board. Write the clue words to find to one side. Invite students prior to and after class to find the words and circle them on the bulletin board.

3. Have students find or draw pictures that they think resemble the people in the book.

4. Invite students to help make an interactive bulletin board quiz. Give each student a half-sheet of paper (about 4"x5") folded in half so that it can open. On the outside flap, have each student write a description of one of the characters in the text. On the inside, they will write the name of the character. You can staple or tack these papers to the bulletin board so that the students can read the descriptions and lift the flaps to find the answers.

5. Collect pictures of Nigeria, past and present.

6. Have students draw book jackets and post them on a bulletin board.

7. Make a display of travel posters of Nigeria and other parts of Africa.

8. Display articles about Chinua Achebe and critiques of his works.

9. Have students design postcards depicting the settings of the book.

10. Display a large world map and have students mark the route that the British probably took to reach Nigeria.

EXTRA ACTIVITIES *Things Fall Apart*

One of the difficulties in teaching a novel is that all students don't read at the same speed. One student who likes to read may take the book home and finish it in a day or two. Sometimes a few students finish the in-class assignments early. The problem, then, is finding suitable extra activities for students.

The best thing I've found is to keep a little library in the classroom. For this unit on *Things Fall Apart,* you might check out from the school or public library other books by Chinua Achebe. There are also many other novels about the colonizing of Africa that students would enjoy reading. Several journals have critiques of Chinua Achebe's works. Some of the students may enjoy reading these and responding either in writing or in discussion groups.

You may want to have good readers make a tape of the book so that your slower readers or students who speak English as a second language can hear the book. At least, make a tape with the pronunciations of the African names and terms.

Chinua Achebe is an interesting person. Your students may enjoy reading a biography of him.

Chinua Achebe grew up in Nigeria, the setting of the novel. Your more able students may want to read his biography, to find out what events in his life influence his writing.

Other things you may keep on hand are word search puzzles. Several puzzles relating directly to *Things Fall Apart* are included in the unit. Feel free to duplicate them.

Some students may like to draw. You might devise a contest or allow some extra-credit grade for students who draw characters or scenes from *Things Fall Apart.* Note, too, that if the students do not want to keep their drawings you may pick up some extra bulletin board materials this way. If you have a contest and you supply the prize, you could, possibly, make the drawing itself a non-refundable entry fee.

Have maps, a globe, and travel brochures on hand for easy reference. Travel agencies and automobile clubs area good sources for these materials.

Show a video about West Africa to acquaint students with its geography and culture.

The pages which follow contain games, puzzles, and worksheets. The keys, when appropriate, immediately follow the puzzle or worksheet. There are two main groups of activities: one group for the unit; that is, generally relating to the *Things Fall Apart* text, and another group of activities related strictly to the *Things Fall Apart* vocabulary.

Directions for the games, puzzles, and worksheets are self-explanatory. The object here is to provide you with extra materials you may use in any way you choose.

MORE ACTIVITIES Things *Fall Apart*

1. Pick one of the incidents for students to dramatize. Encourage students to write dialog for the characters. (Perhaps you could assign various stories to different groups of students so more than one story could be acted and more students could participate.)

2. Have students design a book cover (front and back and inside flaps) for *Things Fall Apart*.

3. Have students design a bulletin board (ready to be put up; not just sketched) for *Things Fall Apart*.

4. Invite a story teller to tell one or more stories related to *Things Fall Apart* to the class.

5. Use some of the related topics (noted earlier for an in-class library) as topics for research, reports, or written papers, or as topics for guest speakers.

6. Help students design and produce a talk show. Choose one of the story incidents as the topic. The host will interview the various characters. (Students should make up the questions they want the host to ask the characters.)

7. Have students work in pairs to create an interview with one of the characters. One student should be the interviewer and the other should be the interviewee. Students can work together to compose questions for the interviewer to ask. Each pair of students could present their interview to the class.

8. Invite students who have read other books by Chinua Achebe to present booktalks to the class.

9. Invite students who have read a biography of Chinua Achebe to tell the class about his life.

10. Invite someone who has lived in one of the areas mentioned in the book to speak to the class.

11. Invite someone who is well-versed in African history to talk to the class.

12. Have students hold small group discussions related to topics in the book. Assign a recorder and a speaker for each group. Have the speaker from each group make a report to the class. want the host to ask the characters.)

THING UNIT

```
C H I E L O Z E L D E K W E F I A W C
B O G H S B B L E E N F O Q B M G R O
R W W C Y E P C G S P O H L N I B E M
O D C R H R T A W P R H M A K A S M
W L N C I U R U A X E O L G E L T I
N G A S Y E K O G I D S F S D M A L S
D N O M R E S W W R M T M F Y E I S
G N W C T X Y D U Y N W M S C F M N I
N C K O W I J Y Z A D I E N A U I G O
B C V S Y L N T K M S S N K L N T X N
U D U E Z E N S T S U C O L P A H J E
B S W C V O W K I V U N C S K A K N R
I C M E H S G O M P U P H I N E J O D
C V S T Z E N B L Q H W R G T D B I Q
Y H Y M B A N T A S S E E E K I A G A
C P P H R T R D P N I D H Q M B X I Y
L G A I F O U M B G C T R Z E Q L L
E B E H L C N Y O N A E A S Y L R E F
M S O K O N K W O M Q R F V F K P R C
```

ACHEBE	ENOCH	MACHETE	PYTHON
AGBALA	EXILE	MBANTA	RELIGION
BICYCLE	EZEUDU	MISSIONARIES	SEVEN
BROWN	FATHER	NWOYE	SMITH
CHIELO	FOREST	OBI	SUPREME
CHUKWU	HANGED	OBIERIKA	UCHENDU
COMMISSIONER	IKEMEFUNA	OGBANGE	UMUOFIA
COWRIES	KIAGA	OKONKWO	UNOKA
DESPAIR	KOLA	ORACLE	WRESTLING
EGWUGWU	LEPROSY	PALM	YAMS
EKWEFI	LOCUSTS	PRISON	

MARY COLLINS

THING UNIT

```
C H I E L O     E L D E K W E F I   A   W C
B O           B   E E   F O         G   R O
R   W C     E P C G S P O     L     I B E M
O     R     C A   W P R     A       K A S M
W     C   E R   A   A   E   O       E L T I
N   A S   E K   R O G I R   S   Y   M A L S
  N O     E S   U W W R   M         E M I S
  N W     X     U   Y A   I   K     F   N I
      O   I     L   A M S E K   A   U   G O
U D U E Z E N S T S U C O L     N   A     N
B   C V O   I   U N C     K A       N   E
I   E H   G M   U P H I   N E       O   R
C S T   E N B L     R G T     B I
Y Y M B A N T A     E E E   K I A G A
C P     R     D P N I D H   M     I
L   A I F O U M U B G C T       E L
E   E           O   A E A           E
      S O K O N K W O M     F       R
```

ACHEBE	ENOCH	MACHETE	PYTHON
AGBALA	EXILE	MBANTA	RELIGION
BICYCLE	EZEUDU	MISSIONARIES	SEVEN
BROWN	FATHER	NWOYE	SMITH
CHIELO	FOREST	OBI	SUPREME
CHUKWU	HANGED	OBIERIKA	UCHENDU
COMMISSIONER	IKEMEFUNA	OGBANGE	UMUOFIA
COWRIES	KIAGA	OKONKWO	UNOKA
DESPAIR	KOLA	ORACLE	WRESTLING
EGWUGWU	LEPROSY	PALM	YAMS
EKWEFI	LOCUSTS	PRISON	

THING UNIT

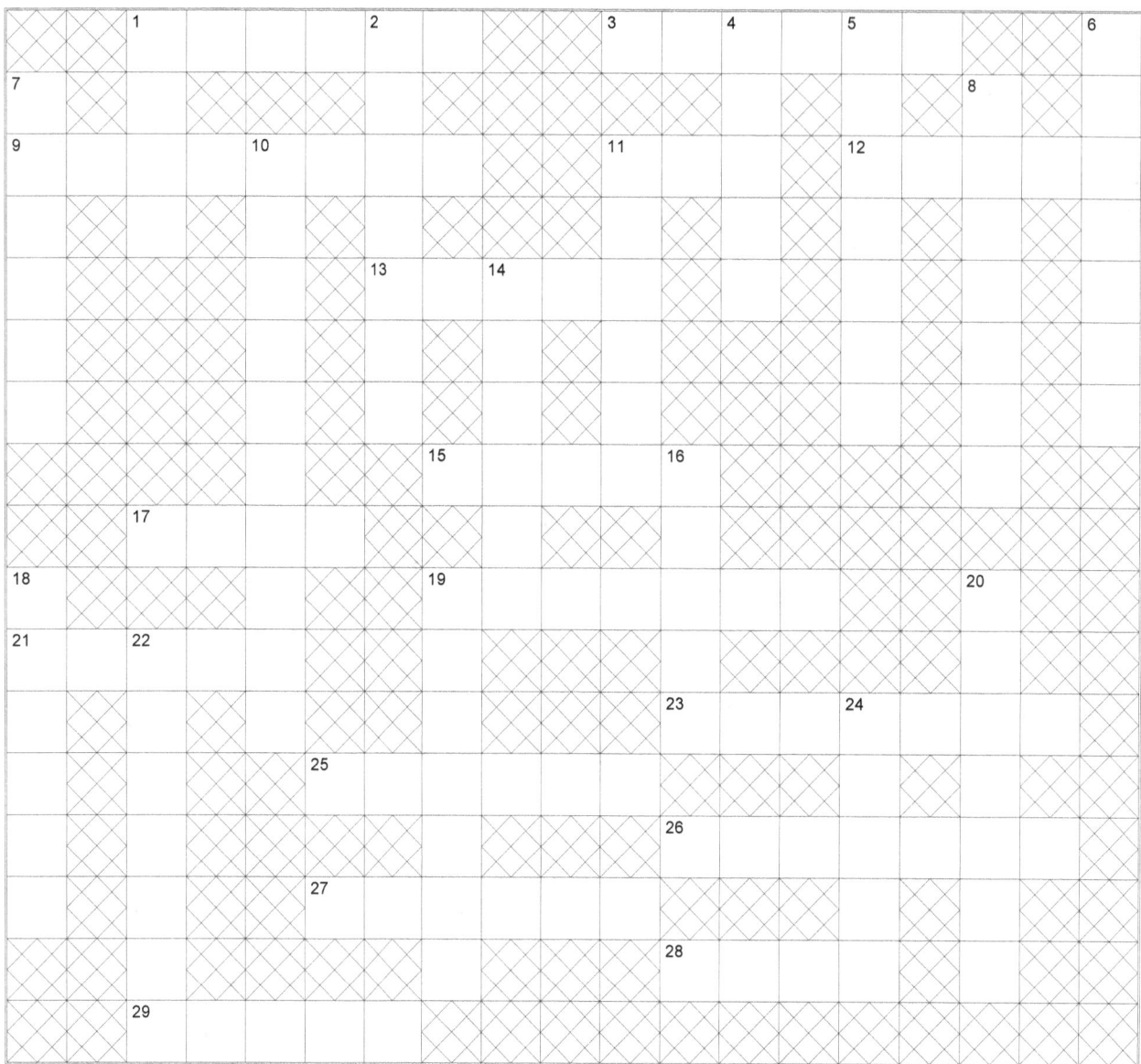

Across
1. Sacred animal
3. Clan elder who had tumultuous funeral
9. What white men brought, along with government
11. Traditional dwelling or hut
12. Mr. Brown's unpleasant successor; Mr. ___
13. In charge of the church in Umuofia after the white man left; Mr. ___
15. Number of years of Okonkwo's exile
17. Major food crop
19. Clan translation for
21. First missionary in Umuofia: Mr. ___
23. Masqueraders who impersonate ancestral spirits
25. The major god of the villagers
26. Okonkwo's home
27. What Ikemefuna called Okonkwo
28. Nuts offered in hospitality
29. Unmasked an egwugwu

Down
1. Type of wine the villagers drank
2. Successful, strong central character of novel
4. Okonkwo's punishment for accidentally shooting the boy
5. What Okonkwo felt when he began his exile
6. Welcomed Okonkwo in Mbanta
7. Where Okonkwo and he others went for destroying the church
8. The iron horse
10. What the white man brought in addition to religion
11. Consulted before decisions were made by the clan
14. Author
16. Okonkwo's son who converted to Christianity
18. Where Okonkwo lived in exile
19. Delicacy caught and roasted by villagers
20. Shells used for money
22. Child who dies and returns to be reborn
24. Okonkwo's unsuccessful father

MARY COLLINS

THING UNIT

Across
1. Sacred animal
3. Clan elder who had tumultuous funeral
9. What white men brought, along with government
11. Traditional dwelling or hut
12. Mr. Brown's unpleasant successor; Mr. ___
13. In charge of the church in Umuofia after the white man left; Mr. ___
15. Number of years of Okonkwo's exile
17. Major food crop
19. Clan translation for
21. First missionary in Umuofia: Mr. ___
23. Masqueraders who impersonate ancestral spirits
25. The major god of the villagers
26. Okonkwo's home
27. What Ikemefuna called Okonkwo
28. Nuts offered in hospitality
29. Unmasked an egwugwu

Down
1. Type of wine the villagers drank
2. Successful, strong central character of novel
4. Okonkwo's punishment for accidentally shooting the boy
5. What Okonkwo felt when he began his exile
6. Welcomed Okonkwo in Mbanta
7. Where Okonkwo and he others went for destroying the church
8. The iron horse
10. What the white man brought in addition to religion
11. Consulted before decisions were made by the clan
14. Author
16. Okonkwo's son who converted to Christianity
18. Where Okonkwo lived in exile
19. Delicacy caught and roasted by villagers
20. Shells used for money
22. Child who dies and returns to be reborn
24. Okonkwo's unsuccessful father

WORKSHEET 1 *Things Fall Apart*

_____ 1. Unoka   A. cautioned Okonkwo not to kill Ikemefuna

_____ 2. Ezinma   B. Okonkso's method of suicide

_____ 3. Obierika   C. Okonkwo's mother's relative

_____ 4. Chielo   D. author Chinua

_____ 5. Mr. Brown   E. many of her children died in infancy

_____ 6. Ekwefi   F. his relatives cleansed Okonkwo's land

_____ 7. *ogbange*   G. saw that things were falling apart

_____ 8. hanged   H. staple crop of villagers

_____ 9. father   I. unsuccessful, debt-laden father

_____ 10. yams   J. white men brought it with religion

_____ 11. machete   K. what Ikemefuna called Okonkwo

_____ 12. wrestling   L. discussed religion with Akunna

_____ 13. Ezeudu   M. ancestral spirit masqueraders

_____ 14. Uchendu   N. Okonkwo used it to kill messenger

_____ 15. obi   O. didn't compromise and accommodate

_____ 16. Mr. Smith   P. evil child who died and was reborn

_____ 17. *egwugwu*   Q. Okonkwo's favorite child

_____ 18. government   R. traditional village hut

_____ 19. Okonkwo   S. took Ezinma to the oracle's cave

_____ 20. Achebe   T. sport enjoyed by villagers

UNIT WORKSHEET - 2 *Things Fall Apart*

_____ 1. prison   A. interpreter in charge of congregation

_____ 2. Nwoye   B. tied to sacred silk-cotton tree

_____ 3. locusts   C. decreed Ikemefuna's fate

_____ 4. Mbanta   D. site of Okonkwo's exile

_____ 5. Ikemefuna   E. visited Okonkwo in exile

_____ 6. Okonkwo   F. clan punishment for accidental killing

_____ 7. bicycle   G. eaten by clan as a delicacy

_____ 8. Christianity   H. strong man full of fear and anger

_____ 9. Agbala   I. taken from Mbaino as retribution

_____ 10. Evil Forest   J. white men brought it and government

_____ 11. oracle   K. white men started one for the natives

_____ 12. seven   L. Oracle of the Hills and Caves

_____ 13. leprosy   M. was writing a book about the "primitives"

_____ 14. Mr. Kiaga   N. sacred animal

_____ 15. python   O. converted to Christianity

_____ 16. commissioner   P. number of years of exile

_____ 17. exile   Q. Christians lived there, to villagers' surprise

_____ 18. Obierika   R. religion brought by the white men

_____ 19. religion   S. definition of "white man"

_____ 20. supreme   T. what mother was, according to Uchendu

ANSWER KEY UNIT WORKSHEETS - *Things Fall Apart*

Worksheet 1
1. I
2. Q
3. A
4. S
5. L
6. E
7. P
8. B
9. K
10. H
11. N
12. T
13. F
14. C
15. R
16. O
17. M
18. J
19. G
20. D

Worksheet 2
1. K
2. O
3. G
4. D
5. I
6. H
7. B
8. R
9. L
10. Q
11. C
12. P
13. S
14. A
15. N
16. M
17. F
18. E
19. J
20. T

JUGGLE WORD GAME - *Things Fall Apart*

SCRAMBLED	WORD	CLUE
EHAECB	ACHEBE	author's last name
ECLBCIY	BICYCLE	the iron horse
LCOHEI	CHIELO	Priestess of the Oracle
PEASRID	DESPAIR	what Okonkwo felt when he began his exile
RSVOITFLEE	EVIL FOREST	where the Christians built their church
LEXIE	EXILE	Okonkwo's punishment for accidentally shooting the boy
MAZENI	ENZINMA	should have been a boy, according to Okonkwo
HARTEF	FATHER	what Ikemefuna called Okonkwo
NDEGAH	HANGED	how Okonkwo killed himself
LOKA	KOLA	nuts offered in hospitality
SRELYOP	LEPROSY	clan translation for "white man"
USTLOCS	LOCUSTS	delicacy caught and roasted by villagers
AMHETCE	MACHETE	weapon Okonwo used to kill the messenger
WEYON	NWOYE	Okonkwo's son who converted to Christianity
BIO	OBI	traditional dwelling or hut
IREBAKOI	OBIERIKA	Okonkwo's friend
NOKWOOK	OKONKWO	successful, strong central character of novel
AEROLRC	ORACLE	consulted before decisions were made by the clan
LAMP	PALM	type of wine the villagers drank
RSONIP	PRISON	Okonkwo was angry when released
NHPYOT	PYTHON	sacred animal
ESNVE	SEVEN	number of years of Okonkwo's exile
FAUOUIM	UMUOFIA	Okonkwo's home
SIRENGLWT	WRESTLING	how Okonkwo won his early fame

VOCABULARY RESOURCE MATERIALS

Things Fall Apart Voc.

```
R T I M A L E V O L E N C E X K T S L
E B M E S O T E R I C O Y P B N J T G
Q D P V T Z D S C O M M U N A L X U E
U E R E B U K E D P P P G E B D Y N M
I R O D I S C E R N A C R R N G H T I
S I V S Y H D O F N J C U T A S F E S
I S I W S E M V D R S O D N I V P D S
T I D W R I L E M I M P L R N S E M A
E V E D S N M R M E G I U J F I B L R
B E N E V O L E N T L O R F R E N Z Y
T I T L N I M S Q Z L U Y T G T I G B
K L S I I T E I W F Q S D O H A N G Q
V S U S M A S L N B V L T E A L T W N
I M O T M N S I T O F Y C P G I E B G
L L I L I A E E U U N A W G T R S B
E P C E N M N N M T W S L K A U V Z S
R K E S E E C T U S V A L O R M A K X
H P P S N L E H L D L N O N D V L D V
G D S R T Z S X T C L P W M X H S B C
```

BEGOT	ELUDE	IMMINENT	OMINOUS
BENEVOLENT	EMANATION	IMPROVIDENT	PANDEMONIUM
BOUTS	EMISSARY	INTERVALS	REBUKED
CALLOW	ESOTERIC	KINDRED	REQUISITE
COMMUNAL	ESSENCES	LISTLESS	RESILIENT
COMPROMISE	FEIGN	MALEVOLENCE	SPECIOUS
COPIOUSLY	FLOURISH	MIRTHLESS	STUNTED
CUNNING	FRENZY	MISCREANT	TUMULT
DERISIVE	GRAVELY	MUTILATE	VALOR
DISCERN	HAGGARD	OMEN	VILE

MARY COLLINS

Things Fall Apart Voc.

```
R   I   M A L E V O L E N C E       T S
E   M   E S O T E R I C O       N   T
Q D P             C O M M U N A L   U E
U E R E B U K E D P   P G E         N M
I R O D I S C E R N A C R       H   T I
S R V     D O     N   C U       A   E S
I S I     E M     D   S O   N   V   D S
T I D   R   E     I   M   R         E A
E V E   S N M R M E   I U   F   I   B R
B E V O L E N T L O R F R E N Z Y
  N L N I M S       L U   T G T   G
K I I I T I     F   S D O H A N   G
V S S M S L N B     L T   A L T     N
I U O T N S I T O     Y C G I E     S
L S I M A E E U U     A   G T R   S
E   C E E M N N M T   S   A U V     S
    E S E   C T   U   S   R M L
    P S N   E     L   L   D   S
    S   T   S     T   W
```

BEGOT   ELUDE   IMMINENT   OMINOUS

BENEVOLENT   EMANATION   IMPROVIDENT   PANDEMONIUM

BOUTS   EMISSARY   INTERVALS   REBUKED

CALLOW   ESOTERIC   KINDRED   REQUISITE

COMMUNAL   ESSENCES   LISTLESS   RESILIENT

COMPROMISE   FEIGN   MALEVOLENCE   SPECIOUS

COPIOUSLY   FLOURISH   MIRTHLESS   STUNTED

CUNNING   FRENZY   MISCREANT   TUMULT

DERISIVE   GRAVELY   MUTILATE   VALOR

DISCERN   HAGGARD   OMEN   VILE

Things Fall Apart Voc.

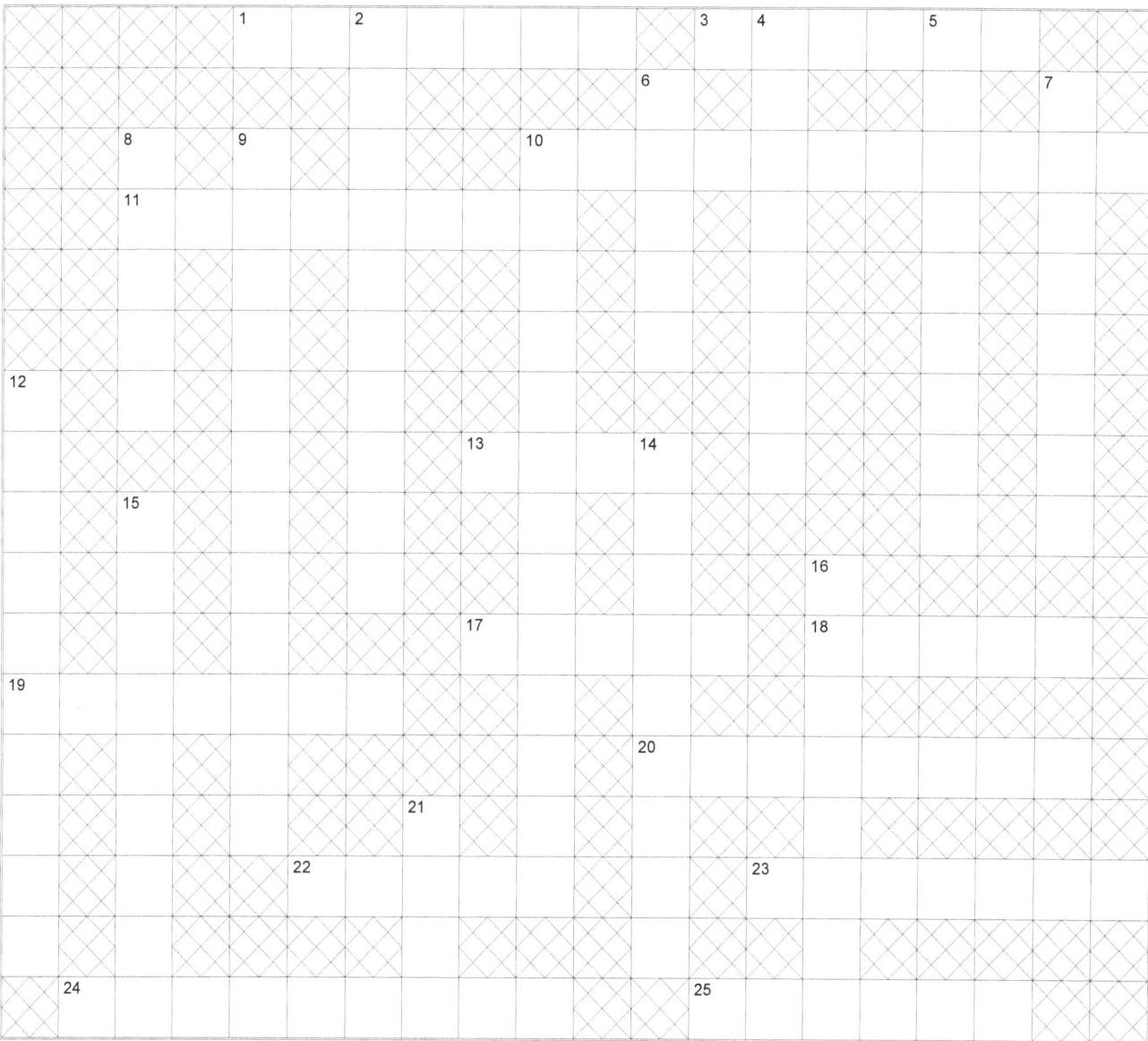

Across
1. Threadlike
3. Youthful; immature
10. Detestable things
11. Known only to the chosen few
13. Prophetic sign
17. Courage and boldness, as in battle; bravery
18. Avoid; evade
19. Skill in deception; guile
20. Impending; near at hand
22. To represent falsely; pretend to
23. Distinguish; perceive
24. Beginning to exist or appear
25. A state of violent mental agitation or wild excitement

Down
2. Characterized by or suggestive of doing good
4. Stirred up; disturbed
5. Exclude from public favor
6. A contest between antagonists; a match
7. Of a group of people
8. Produced; fathered
9. Payment or reimbursement
10. Help; adaptation
12. Impulsive and unpredictable
14. Known widely and usually unfavorably
15. Issuing forth
16. Ridiculing
21. Disgusting; loathsome

Things Fall Apart Voc.

Across
1. Threadlike
3. Youthful; immature
10. Detestable things
11. Known only to the chosen few
13. Prophetic sign
17. Courage and boldness, as in battle; bravery
18. Avoid; evade
19. Skill in deception; guile
20. Impending; near at hand
22. To represent falsely; pretend to
23. Distinguish; perceive
24. Beginning to exist or appear
25. A state of violent mental agitation or wild excitement

Down
2. Characterized by or suggestive of doing good
4. Stirred up; disturbed
5. Exclude from public favor
6. A contest between antagonists; a match
7. Of a group of people
8. Produced; fathered
9. Payment or reimbursement
10. Help; adaptation
12. Impulsive and unpredictable
14. Known widely and usually unfavorably
15. Issuing forth
16. Ridiculing
21. Disgusting; loathsome

VOCABULARY WORKSHEET 1 - *Things Fall Apart*

____ 1. DETESTABLE THINGS
    A. abominations   B. calabashes   C. essences   D. spectators

____ 2. CONTESTS, MATCHES
    A. emanations   B. capricious   C. bouts   D. consolations

____ 3. MENTAL CALMNESS
    A. diffused   B. composure   C. brusqueness   D. cunning

____ 4. ABUNDANTLY
    A. copiously   B. agitated   C. derisive   D. notorious

____ 5. RIDICULING
    A. miscreant   B. mirthless   C. haggard   D. derisive

____ 6. EXPRESSIVE, PERSUASIVE
    A. provoking   B. resilient   C. eloquent   D. stunted

____ 7. AVOID; EVADE
    A. imperious   B. elude   C. rebuked   D. incipient

____ 8. REPRESENTATIVE SENT IN ADVANCE
    A. emissary   B. emanation   C. kindred   D. callow

____ 9. GROW WELL; PROSPER
    A. incipient   B. frenzy   C. discern   D. flourish

____ 10. THREADLIKE
    A. fibrous   B. copiously   C. specious   D. notorious

____ 11. SERIOUSLY
    A. gravely   B. provoking   C. imminent   D. resilient

____ 12. FORERUNNERS
    A. spectators   B. harbingers   C. calabashes   D. kindred

____ 13. STIMULATING OR EXCITING
    A. manifest   B. ominous   C. intoxicating   D. perpetual

____ 14. PROPHETIC SIGN
    A. resignation   B. omen   C. miscreant   D. flourish

____ 15. WILD UPROAR OR NOISE
    A. requisite   B. abomination   C. capricious   D. pandemonium

____ 16. LASTING FOR ETERNITY
    A. perpetual   B. discordant   C. esoteric   D. imminent

____ 17. UNRESISTING; PATIENTLY SUBMISSIVE
    A. specious   B. begot   C. resignation   D. benevolent

____ 18. COMMOTION; RIOT
    A. haggard   B. resilient   C. feign   D. tumult

____ 19. SEEMINGLY RELIABLE BUT INCORRECT
    A. impenetrably   B. malevolence   C. specious   D. incipient

____ 20. COURAGE AND BOLDNESS
    A. feign   B. valor   C. prestige   D. profound

VOCABULARY WORKSHEET 2 - *Things Fall Apart*

____ 1. agitated   A. understandable, clear

____ 2. brusqueness   B. lacking in spirit or energy

____ 3. capricious   C. to disfigure or deprive of a limb

____ 4. compromise   D. relating to a clan or tribe

____ 5. delectable   E. impulsive and unpredictable

____ 6. derisive   F. necessary requirement

____ 7. discern   G. deep; complete

____ 8. emissary   H. appearing worn and exhausted

____ 9. fibrous   I. not able to be entered or pierced

____ 10. haggard   J. amount of time between two specified instances

____ 11. impenetrably   K. greatly disturbed

____ 12. intervals   L. threatening

____ 13. kindred   M. delightful; delicious

____ 14. listless   N. threadlike

____ 15. manifest   O. distinguish; perceive

____ 16. mutilate   P. agent sent in advance

____ 17. ominous   Q. stirred up; disturbed

____ 18. perturbed   R. ridiculing

____ 19. profound   S. discourteously blunt

____ 20. requisite   T. adjustment

ANSWER KEY VOCABULARY WORKSHEETS - *Things Fall Apart*

Worksheet 1
1. A
2. C
3. B
4. A
5. D
6. C
7. B
8. A
9. D
10. A
11. A
12. B
13. C
14. B
15. D
16. A
17. C
18. D
19. C
20. B

Worksheet 2
1. Q
2. S
3. E
4. T
5. M
6. R
7. O
8. P
9. N
10. H
11. I
12. J
13. D
14. B
15. A
16. C
17. L
18. K
19. G
20. F

VOCABULARY REVIEW GAME - *Things Fall Apart*

SCRAMBLED	WORD	CLUE
MONTAISABON	ABOMINATIONS	detestable things
ETTGDAIA	AGITATED	stirred up; disturbed
TOGEB	BEGOT	produced; fathered
TUBOS	BOUTS	a contest between antagonists; a match
HSSBCAAEAL	CALABASHES	utensils made from dried gourds
OWLCAL	CALLOW	youthful; immature
RAICUPCISO	CAPRICIOUS	impulsive and unpredictable
OUCAMMLN	COMMUNAL	of a group of people
MORESOUPC	COMPOSURE	mental calmness
GINUCNN	CUNNING	skill in deception; guile
IIEDERSV	DERISIVE	ridiculing
CERSNDI	DISCERN	distinguish; perceive
RAMSYSIE	EMISSARY	an agent sent to advance the interests of another
RECITSEO	ESOTERIC	known only to the chosen few
NIGEF	FEIGN	to represent falsely; pretend to
BUFIOSR	FIBROUS	threadlike
LORHUSFI	FLOURISH	grow well; prosper
EYRZNF	FRENZY	a state of violent mental agitation
YGREVAL	GRAVELY	seriously
NEINTPCII	INCIPIENT	beginning to exist or appear
VIALSTNRE	INTERVALS	amount of time between specified instances
NEDKDRI	KINDRED	related to a clan or tribe
ESSILSLT	LISTLESS	lacking in spirit or energy
STEFIMAN	MANIFEST	understandable; clear
NOEM	OMEN	prophetic sign
TPREAREUP	PERPETUAL	lasting for eternity
ETBERDRPU	PERTURBED	greatly disturbed
UTTLUM	TUMULT	commotion; riot
LAROV	VALOR	courage and boldness
LIVE	VILE	disgusting; loathsome

www.ingramcontent.com/pod-product-compliance
Lightning Source LLC
Chambersburg PA
CBHW051414070526
44584CB00023B/3430